EVERYONE'S GUIDE *to*

Angels

D0027273

CHARISMA
HOUSE

Most CHARISMA HOUSE BOOK GROUP products are available at special quantity discounts for bulk purchase for sales promotions, premiums, fund-raising, and educational needs. For details, write Charisma House Book Group, 600 Rinehart Road, Lake Mary, Florida 32746, or telephone (407) 333-0600.

EVERYONE'S GUIDE TO ANGELS edited by Charisma House
Published by Charisma House
Charisma Media/Charisma House Book Group
600 Rinehart Road
Lake Mary, Florida 32746
www.charismahouse.com

Cover design by Vincent Pirozzi
Design Director: Justin Evans

Library of Congress Cataloging-in-Publication Data:
Everyone's guide to angels / Charisma House Editors.
     pages cm
  Includes bibliographical references.
  ISBN 978-1-62998-211-3 (trade paper) -- ISBN 978-1-62998-252-6 (e-book)
  1. Angels. I. Charisma House.
  BT966.3.E94 2015
  235'.3--dc23

                                              2015006721

This publication is translated in Spanish under the title *Una guía esencial para los ángeles*, copyright © 2015 published by Casa Creación, a Charisma Media company. All rights reserved.

PART I

All About Angels

Chapter 1

WHAT ARE ANGELS?

By Terry Law

TO SOME PEOPLE, the very existence of angels is in question. To them, no proof may be possible, though evidence may abound. Yet if you place confidence in Scripture, it is clear that the angels who appear from beginning to end are not symbols, figures of speech, or mental illusions. They are individual beings created by God, and they share in His plan for mankind or oppose it with Satan as their leader.

Accepting the existence of angels raises many other questions about them:

- Where did angels come from?

- How many are there?

- What is their nature?

- What do they look like?

- How much power and authority do they have over the earth and its inhabitants?

- What is their position in relation to mankind?

- What is their position in relation to Jesus?

The word *angel* simply means "messenger." The Hebrew word is *malakh*, and the Greek is *angelos*. Depending on the context, these words can indicate a human messenger (1 Sam. 6:21; Isa. 44:26;

Matt. 11:10; Luke 7:24; James 2:25) or the supernatural heavenly beings we call angels (Luke 1:11; Ps. 104:4; Matt. 4:6; Rev. 16:1).[1]

THE ORIGIN OF ANGELS

The psalmist understood that God created the angels (Ps. 103:20–21; 148:2). In the New Testament, the apostle Paul wrote to the church at Colossae in what is now Turkey:

> For by Him all things were created that are in heaven and that are in earth, visible and invisible, whether they are thrones, or dominions, or principalities, or powers. All things were created by Him and for Him.
> —COLOSSIANS 1:16

One of the errors Paul was writing about to the Colossians was the worship of angels. Some scholars think this was part of a Judaistic Gnosticism, a forerunner of the full-blown gnostic religion of the third century.

Also, it is obvious from this verse that Jesus is not the first and highest angel, as some New Age and other non-Christian systems teach. Paul wrote that by Him were all things created, and that includes angels. Paul told them it was misguided humility to bow down to angels (Col. 2:18). Angels are created beings, not divine.

There are differences of opinion as to exactly when the creation of angels took place in relation to the creation of man. Here are two different ideas:

1. Angels were created before man when God created the heavens and the earth (Gen. 1:1). This involves the "gap theory" or the "ruin-reconstruction" theory, which presents the idea that there is an indefinite time gap between verses 1 and 2 of Genesis 1. This theory, or doctrine, says God created a perfect world some time in the unknown past. When Satan rebelled (Isa. 14), the

inhabitants of that world fell with him. Judgment, or warfare, resulted in the earth becoming chaotic. According to the theory, the plants, animals, and beings of that time, whose fossils are found today, are genetically unrelated to today's earth or to human beings.

2. Angels were not created before the universe but during the "hexaemeron"—the six epochs or eras of creation represented by six days in Scripture. Only God existed before the creation of the universe (Gen. 2:2–3).[2]

After studying Scripture and the various theological positions on this, it seems to me that angels must have been created before the universe, when there was only God Himself. One verse in the Bible literally spells out that angels were already there when God created the earth.

> Where were you when I laid the foundations of the earth…when the morning stars sang together, and all the sons of God shouted for joy?
> —Job 38:4–7

The phrase "sons of God" is used several times in Scripture to refer to angels. Also, it is obvious that Satan existed before God created Adam and Eve, and that he is an angelic being.

All angels were created holy, because God said that everything He had created was "good" (Gen. 1:21). God could not be all good and directly create anything wicked.

Angels were not only holy in nature (Mark 8:38), but everything and every influence in their surroundings were good. They had great privileges—one of them being direct, personal fellowship with God. However, God granted angels the ability to make choices, and some angels chose to rebel with Satan.

According to the Bible, those angels who followed Satan cannot be redeemed (Matt. 25:41). Some theologians suggest the

rebellious angels may have had a period of probation when they
could have repented.

But why would God provide redemption for the sons of Adam
but not for angels? The late Henry Clarence Theissen, first dean
of Wheaton College, wrote:

> Because angels are a company and not a race, they sinned
> individually, and not in some federal head of the race (like
> Adam). It may be that because of this, God made no provi-
> sion of salvation for the fallen angels.[3]

Why Did God Create Angels?

Thomas Aquinas, a medieval scholar who was called the "angelic
doctor" because he wrote about angels so much, suggested that
angels had to be created in order to "perfect" the universe. In
other words, if everything that could exist was not created, then
creation would not be perfect, which would be impossible for God.

Another theory is that God is a God of "order," and an unfilled
gap would upset the order of the universe. This is called the "great
chain of being" theory. This thought, carried to the extreme, led
to the idea that God had to be approached through intermediaries.

A third idea is that God created angels to praise Him, show
Him honor, and bring Him glory. The very name for this order of
beings—messengers—also seems to imply that they were created
for a certain function.

However, it seems to me that all of the theories about why God
created angels can be put to rest with one statement: He did it
because He wanted to! It really is not necessary—and may not be
our business—to understand why He wanted to.

One thing we can observe is that each angel appears to have
been a direct creation of God, says Robert Lightner of Dallas
Theological Seminary.[4] In contrast, for the beginning of mankind, God created an original pair that could reproduce. Men
and angels have different natures because they were created in
different ways.

The result of this, according to Theissen, is that angels are a company, not a race, and are considered an "order" of creation. That means angels do not procreate—at least, they do not procreate in their natural state.[5] They are called "sons of God" in the sense of having been created by God, but they are never called "sons of angels."[6] Angels do not die (Luke 20:36), so the number God created has, and will, remain the same.

How Many Angels Are There?

The number of angels that exist was a popular subject for theologians during the Middle Ages despite the fact that they never did argue over how many angels could stand on the head of a pin.

Jewish mystics in the Middle Ages came up with 301,655,722 angels, a number arrived at by a complicated formula of assigning numbers to letters, translating the letters back to numbers, and counting them. Author and publisher John Ronner wrote that no matter how many there are, angels "outnumber us like the Sioux nation did Custer at the Little Big Horn!"[7]

One Scripture verse mentions "ten thousand times ten thousand," which would be a hundred million in that one place (Dan. 7:10). The bottom line of these allusions seems to be that angels are innumerable (Heb. 12:22). Or, as Elisha told his servant, "They that be with us are more than they that be with them" (2 Kings 6:16, KJV).

However, Job had the perfect answer to questions about the number of angels: "Who is able to number his hosts of angels?" (Job 25:3, TLB).

If we cannot know how many angels there are, can we know what angels are like? What kind of natures do they have, since each one is a separate creation and not a race with inherited characteristics as is man?

The Nature and Appearance of Angels

It is generally recognized that there are three elements or attributes of personality, all of which are possessed by angels:

1. Angels have intelligence, which is expressed
   through a desire to look into the salvation of
   humans (1 Pet. 1:12) and by the ability to commu-
   nicate intelligently in speech. In fact, they apparently have their own languages (1 Cor. 13:1).

   Writers of all systematic theologies, both Protestant and Catholic, call angels "rational" beings.
   Angels have wisdom as well as knowledge that is
   beyond man's about many matters. Second Samuel
   14:20 says, "My lord is wise, as with the wisdom of
   the angel of God, so as to discern everything happening in the land."

   We also can infer that angels render intelligent
   worship to God from passages throughout Scripture and especially the Book of Revelation. However, there is nothing in the Bible that would lead
   us to believe that some angels are more intelligent
   than others. Apparently, they were not created
   with all the knowledge they ever would have, but
   from inferences in Scripture they are growing in
   knowledge (Eph. 3:9–10; 1 Pet. 1:12).

2. Angels have emotions, which we see by their
   rejoicing over a sinner who is saved (Luke 15:10)
   and their exuberant celebration at the birth of
   Jesus.

3. Angels have wills. They have the ability to choose
   from various courses of action and to follow
   through. In the case of Lucifer and the angels who
   followed him, some angels exercised their wills by
   rebelling against God.

It seems evident from the examples of angels in the Bible that
they definitely have personalities. But what does the Bible say
about what angels look like?

Despite being individually created (which means God could

have created them exactly alike), there seem to be differences between certain orders of angelic beings. Messenger angels do not look like cherubim and vice versa.

Roland Buck, my friend who described many personal incidents of angelic visitations, said:

> Everyone seems to be interested in knowing something about the physical appearance of angels. No two of them look alike! They are different sizes, have different hairstyles, and completely different appearances.[8]

Angels' bodies are not discussed in the Bible. However, this question has been the subject of much discussion and debate over the years in the church, particularly during the Middle Ages. Do they have bodies at all? Or are they pure spirit beings?

In stories our ministry has collected, there have been angels with wings and angels without wings, angels who appear as angels and angels who appear as human beings.

It seems likely to me that angels who appear to us as men, not as angels, would look like the people to whom they are appearing. In other words, if the angel who appeared to Samson's mother had not looked like an Israelite, would she have called him "a man of God" as if he were an Israelite prophet (Judg. 13:6)?

If angels "appear unawares" (Heb. 13:2, KJV), then angels are appearing as Chinese to Chinese and African to Africans, as well as American to Americans. That would mean there are angels appearing as blacks as well as whites—probably as every nationality of the world.

The Bible does not tell us that all angels have wings. This idea of wings comes from a verse in Daniel where it says an angel was "caused to fly swiftly" (Dan. 9:21). However, as angels do not move through space and time as we do, we do not know that they need wings to fly. The fact remains that people who report seeing angels often observe that they have wings.

Other orders of heavenly beings called cherubim, seraphim, and living creatures are described with wings (Ezek. 1:5–11, 1 Kings

6:27). In medieval art, many angels were drawn with wings, but they were based on the Greek goddess Nike. Therefore, I believe many angels probably do not have wings.

Both the Roman Catholic Church and Protestants agree that angels do not have material bodies. They are "pure spirits, not composed of matter and form, but composed of essence and existence, of act and potentiality," wrote Aquinas.[9]

In non-Christian religions, the idea of how angels look varies, particularly with specific angelic personalities as they are perceived or imagined by different groups.

We are not usually aware of their presence because angels do not make visible appearances the majority of the time. Hope Price, author of *Angels: True Stories of How They Touch Our Lives*, quotes a Suffolk, England, minister as saying:

> Angels tend to be shy creatures. They are messengers and so do not flaunt themselves. If at all possible, they do not appear.[10]

Are they shy? Or are real angels concerned that people might focus on them? Are angels aware of the human propensity to worship creatures instead of the Creator? Do they realize that the glory of their appearance can cause such fear that their message is overshadowed?

Billy Graham was asked, "What would I see if I saw an angel?" His answer was:

> God is forever imaginative, colorful, and glorious in what He designs. Some of the descriptions of angels, including the one of Lucifer in Ezekiel 28, indicate that they are exotic to the human eye and mind. Apparently angels have a beauty and variety that surpass anything known to men.[11]

Angels in Scripture appear in masculine form, and the word *angel* is always in the masculine gender. Nowhere in the Bible do we read of a feminine angel. Even when they appeared to people as humans ("angels unawares"), it was always in the form of men, not women.

The Speed of Angels

I have always been fascinated with the difference between an earthly body and a spirit body. In an earthly body of flesh and blood, we are restricted. We can travel only at certain speeds, such as in the pressurized compartment of a military jet or spacecraft. If the speed (g-forces) were to be increased, the pressure would peel the flesh from our bodies. We are also unable to move through solids, such as a wall. The spirit world, however, is not limited to human restrictions. Angels are spirits and can move faster than the speed of light.

Ezekiel saw cherubim moving in the heavens and said they "ran back and forth, in appearance like a flash of lightning" (Ezek. 1:13–14). Light travels at 186,000 miles per second. The earth is approximately 25,000 miles in circumference at the equator. This means that light could travel around the earth nearly 7.5 times in just one second (186,000 miles per second divided by 25,000). In the earthly realm, if angels can travel at the speed of light, then they can arrive on the scene in your time of difficulty the moment you say, "Help!"

Let me add that a spirit is not restricted to walls, doors, or other objects. Even Christ in His resurrected body could walk through a door that was locked (John 20:19). There is one type of transportation faster than the speed of light, and it's the speed of thought. The spirit world can actually travel at the speed of thought, which is presently impossible to determine. Angelic beings can be at the throne in heaven and immediately be in the atmosphere above the earth. When the angel appeared to Daniel and informed him that for twenty-one days the answer to his prayer had been hindered by a demonic spirit in the air, the angel said, "Since the first day you began to pray...your request has been heard in heaven. I have come in answer to your prayer" (Dan. 10:12, NLT). Daniel's words ascended from Babylon and were heard the same day in heaven. The angel was coming on the same day to bring the answer but was restrained by the evil prince spirit over Persia (Dan. 10:13). Angels can travel from the highest part of the heaven at the edge of the universe to Earth and back by simply thinking about where they desire to go.

—PERRY STONE, *Angels on Assignment*

THE POWER AND AUTHORITY OF ANGELS

Angels are greater than mankind in might and power (2 Pet. 2:11). They are not all-powerful as God is, but unusual strength is attributed to them (Ps. 103:20; Matt. 28:2). Certain elements of nature are under angelic control at certain times (Rev. 7:1; 14:18).

Their powers are derived from God and exercised in accordance with the laws of the material and spiritual world:

- They rolled back a stone that could have weighed two tons (Luke 24:2–4).

- They closed the mouths of lions (Dan. 6:22).

- They opened prison doors and loosed chains (Acts 12:7–10).

Fred Dickason, author of *Angels: Elect and Evil*, commented that even though angels have powers that are different from ours, God limits what they can do. Yet He does permit them some latitude in how they deal with the people to whom they are sent. Apparently, the higher the rank, the more delegated authority they have on which to act.[12]

I believe one example of an angel exercising the authority God gave him is in the meeting between Gabriel and the priest Zacharias. It is unlikely that God had told Gabriel to strike Zacharias dumb for months if Zacharias responded with unbelief. Gabriel had the latitude to handle such things as he saw fit. In the end, when the baby arrived and they named him what the angel had said, Zacharias's speech was restored (Luke 1:20, 64). The result was much glory and honor given to God, which is always the aim of the angels.

Angels of Light

To whatever degree it exists, pride hinders discernment, and without discernment, we accept counterfeits. An "angel of light" in biblical terms is not an angel that appears in a burst of light or looks radiant or has a halo around his head. An angel of light, regardless of what he looks like, says, or does, is a spirit who presents a gospel other than what is found in the Bible. (See 2 Corinthians 11:14–15 and Galatians 1:8.)

The one real standard we have for knowing whether an angel is an angel of God or an angel of light is whether or not his words and actions match Scripture. An angel of God is most concerned with furthering God's purposes on earth. Therefore, any other purpose or result of an angelic visit should cause immediate suspicion of the presence of an angel of light instead.

One young woman told how she was depressed from a traumatic emotional experience and cried out for divine help. Later she woke and saw the beams of her bedroom ceiling glowing in the shape of a large golden cross. A voice said, "Fear ye not, I am the Lord."

Later she began to have psychic experiences and dreams about what she described as her past lives (reincarnation).[13] The result of the woman's golden-cross vision was not a closer walk with God but an acceptance of "another gospel." Because of her experiences, she also started to give other people spiritual advice.

It is when we feel the most desperate that we must be on our guard against temptations from Satan. When this woman had an encounter with the supernatural, she accepted it as from God without judging the experience according to Scripture. I believe she was deceived by an angel of light.

What can protect us from being deceived? Bank tellers, learning to distinguish counterfeit money from the genuine item, do not major on the counterfeit. They study the real thing until they cannot accept a "dollar of light" as a real buck. In the same manner we need to study God's Word and learn His ways so we will recognize Satan's counterfeits.

In addition, there is no substitute for walking close enough to the Lord in prayer to be able to get what some Christians call "a check" or "a witness" from the Holy Spirit. These "red lights" and "green lights" tell us whether something we are hearing or reading is the real thing. Then we can investigate the matter further to find out what is right or wrong with it.

Angels of God often appear in the Bible as God's messengers. Angels of light carry messages, too, but they are not from God. Their lies started two major religions that are practiced today: Islam and Mormonism.

—Terry Law

THE RELATIONSHIP OF JESUS, ANGELS, AND MAN

Both people and angels are responsible to obey and serve God, and all will be held accountable to Him. We may look at the greater wisdom, knowledge, and power of the angels and think of ourselves as inferior. Yet, angels are curious about us.

- They want to understand redemption (1 Pet. 1:12).

- They observe the affairs of the redeemed (1 Cor. 4:9; 11:10; 1 Tim. 5:21).

- They are to gain a better understanding of God's wisdom as it is displayed through the church (Eph. 3:9–10).

- They know when the lost become "found" by God and rejoice over their salvation (Luke 15:10).

- They apparently stay busy ministering to people in various ways, yet we do not have to do anything for angels.

In Jesus's future kingdom, there is no mention that angels will rule and reign with Him, yet we will (2 Tim. 2:12; Rev. 5:10; 20:6; 22:5).

Theologian Lewis Chafer said angels are called "sons of God" in the Old Testament, while men are called "servants of God." This is reversed in the New Testament. He says this may be because in the New Testament, saints are seen in relation to "their final exaltation into the likeness of Christ compared to which estate, the angels are inferior."[14]

It seems the bottom line is that both angels and born-again human beings were designed to be servants of God, but only man is called a "child" of God through a blood covenant. In the Old Testament angels are called "sons of God," but the relationship is quite different from being a child of God through the blood of Jesus (Heb. 9:14–15).

JESUS COMPARED TO ANGELS

The Book of Hebrews contrasts the relative positions of Jesus and angels very carefully. Angels were held in high regard by the Jews of Jesus's day, which is why the author of Hebrews addressed this question.

Hebrews 1:5–14 demonstrates that Christ is superior to angels in the dignity of His position.

- He is God's only begotten Son.

- He is the Son of David, who inherited and fulfilled God's promise to David.

- He is the reigning Son of man.

- His throne is higher than the angels.

- He is eternal and not a created being. Although angels do not die, they have not always existed, as the Bible tells us Jesus has.

- He is the victorious King and Priest, while angels are "ministering spirits" assigned to render service to those who accept the salvation provided by Jesus.

- He is ruler of the kingdom of God, while angels are not assigned dominion. We see that only the begotten Son of God could overcome Satan and his fallen angels. On the cross, Jesus defeated and judged all the evil angelic forces arrayed against God (John 12:31–33; 16:11; Heb. 2:14).

Because of that, Jesus is declared Lord over all, and every knee in heaven, on earth, and under the earth will bow to Him, and every tongue will confess that He is Lord to the glory of God (Phil. 2:9–11). We are never to worship angels, but rather we are to join with the angels in worshipping Jesus.

Hitchhiking With an Angel

One time I bought a pickup truck, and it was just one of those things for me—it was my dream vehicle. I really wanted it. I told myself, "God wants me to have it. I'm going to save my money, and when I get enough money, I'll be able to buy this pickup truck." At the time I just loved trucks, so when I saw this particular pickup in the paper—and it was a really great price, like $3,000 below wholesale—I thought, "This is it!"

But first a little backstory. I had a friend who had seen a Mercedes-Benz for sale in the paper for $500. He went to the woman who advertised it and said, "I know this has to be a mistake. I know you're really selling it for $50,000." But she said, "No. It really is $500." When he asked her what was wrong with it, she said, "Nothing. It's perfect. It's in mint condition, but my husband has run away with his secretary and has told me to sell the car and send him the money I get for it. So I'm selling the car for $500, and I'm going to send him the money."

So when I saw the pickup truck in the paper for $3,000 under wholesale, I thought, "This is like that! I'm going to get this truck!" I went to look it over, and it was all shiny and clean. It had everything that I wanted. So I paid the money and got the truck.

I decided to drive it to West Texas where I was invited to speak at a church. At one point I'd driven so far I hadn't seen anything for twenty miles. Not even a cow. It was desolate. Nothing is going on. And that's when my truck started slowing down. I pushed on the gas, but it slowed down to nothing. I looked in the mirror and saw smoke billowing out from under the truck, and I realized I had blown the transmission.

It had burned up. And there I am in the middle of desolate West Texas. There was nothing and no one.

"Lord," I asked, "why did You allow this to happen? I'm Your servant. I am going to speak at this church. I have to be there tonight. I'm speaking tonight. Why are You letting this happen to me?"

And the Lord spoke back to me. He said, "I didn't tell you to buy this truck."

"But Lord," I answered, "it was the right price. It was everything I wanted."

"I didn't tell you to buy this truck," He repeated.

"Well, Lord, OK, I'm sorry. I am. I'm sorry I bought it," I replied. "But, Lord, help me. I have got to be at the church tonight. Please help me."

I had not even finished praying that prayer when over a little rise in the road came an old, old, like 1960s, car. It was just puttering along. A man was driving who looked like a farmer. He stopped, looked at me, and said, "Boy, it's not your lucky day is it?"

"No, sir, it's not," I said. "I made a mistake buying this truck."

"Well, I reckon you did," he said. "Where are you going?"

"You don't know the place," I told him, assuming he wouldn't. "I'm going to this little town called Floydada, Texas."

"I know exactly where it's at," he said. "I'm going right through there, son. Hop in, and I'll take you."

So I got in, and he drove me to Floydada, Texas. He dropped me off at the church, and when I get out of his car, I took two steps up onto the sidewalk and turned around to thank him, and…he was gone.

I mean, the car was gone. The man was gone. There was nothing. The car wasn't driving away; it was just gone. Two seconds, two steps. He was gone.

I had entertained an angel "unaware," as the Scripture says—until that very moment when I looked back and realized, "Oh my goodness. That was an angel."

—JOHN PAUL JACKSON, AUTHOR AND FOUNDER OF ENCOUNTERS NETWORK

THE NATURE OF ANGELS

By James W. Goll

*T*HE EXISTENCE OF angels has been acknowledged by people of many cultures and many religions throughout all of human civilization. In other words, the Judeo-Christian tradition cannot lay sole claim to them. But we can lay claim to having the closest association with them because we are laboring together with them to bring the rule and reign of God's kingdom to the world.

Above all, angels exist to serve God. The very name *angel* denotes one of their functions, that of being a "messenger" of God. Here is how St. Augustine, influential preacher and father of the church, described angels in a sermon he preached in northern Africa at the end of the fourth century. His comments are quoted by the late Catholic theologian Pascal Parente:

> "The Angels are spirits," says Saint Augustine, "but it is not because they are spirits that they are Angels. They become Angels when they are sent, for the name Angel refers to their office not to their nature. You ask the name of this nature, it is *spirit;* you ask its office, it is that of an Angel, (i.e., a messenger). In as far as he exists, an Angel is a spirit; in as far as he acts, he is an Angel." The word "angel" comes from a Greek word meaning "messenger." In the Scriptures of the Old Testament, the most frequently used [Hebrew] name to designate the Angels is *mal'akh,* which means messenger or legate.
>
> This generic name, "angel," does not reveal anything about the real nature of those celestial beings besides the fact

> that they are occasionally sent on a mission as messengers or legates of God to men...They have been given the name of messengers from the most common duty and office they fulfill towards God's children here on earth. "And of the angels he saith, 'Who maketh his angels spirits, and his ministers a flame of fire'" [Heb. 1:7, KJV].[1]

Angels are not omniscient (all knowing), omnipresent (all present), or omnipotent (all powerful), as God is. But they are a lot more knowledgeable, available, and powerful than we are. In fact, a great deal of our experience of God's glorious, powerful presence depends on the angels who convey it and display it to us. Human beings exist to serve God too, but we are much more limited in our supernatural reach than our coworkers, the angels, are.

MORE WAYS OF DEFINING ANGELS

In the many books that have been written about angels, they are described in a variety of ways. Here is a sampling of what others have said about the nature of these celestial beings known as angels:

Martin Luther, German reformer (1483–1546): "An angel is a spiritual creature created by God without a body, for the service of Christendom and of the church."[2]

John Calvin, French reformer (1509–1564): "In Scripture, then, we uniformly read that angels are heavenly spirits, whose obedience and ministry God employs to execute all the purposes which he has decreed, and hence their name as being a kind of intermediate messengers to manifest his will to men. The names by which several of them are distinguished have reference to the same office. They are called hosts, because they surround their Prince as his court,—adorn and display his majesty,—like soldiers, have their eyes always turned to their leader's standard, and are so ready and prompt to execute his orders, that the moment he gives the nod, they prepare for, or rather are actually at work...As his government of the world is exercised and administered by them, they are called at one time Principalities, at another Powers, at another Dominions (Col. 1:16; Eph. 1:21)...

"...Angels are the ministers and dispensers of the divine bounty towards us. Accordingly, we are told how they watch for our safety, how they undertake our defence, direct our path, and take heed that no evil befall us...The protection of those whom he [the Lord] has undertaken to defend he has delegated to his angels...

"...Angels are ministering spirits (Heb. 1:14); whose service God employs for the protection of his people, and by whose means he distributes his favours among men, and also executes other works."[3]

Contemporary, cross-traditional perspective: This is quoted from a book by Margaret Barker, a Methodist preacher who is the former president of the Society for Old Testament Study and a Hebrew scholar: "'Angel' means messenger, and humans experience angels primarily as messengers. But this is not what they 'are;' this is what they do. Angels exist to praise God and humans who experience their presence are being guided toward this universal hymn of praise. Mystics and seers have heard their song, and those who respond to the angels' message move inevitably toward the harmony the angels represent, the 'peace on earth' of the Bethlehem angels. By joining the song of the angels, human hearts and minds are connected to the power of the invisible creation, and their lives are renewed."[4]

Billy Graham, spokesman for twentieth-century evangelicalism: "Angels belong to a uniquely different dimension of creation that we, limited to the natural order, can scarcely comprehend. In this angelic domain the limitations are different from those God has imposed on our natural order. He has given angels higher knowledge, power and mobility than we...They are God's messengers whose chief business is to carry out His orders in the world. He has given them an ambassadorial charge. He has designated and empowered them as holy deputies to perform works of righteousness. In this way they assist Him as their creator while

He sovereignly controls the universe. So He has given them the capacity to bring His holy enterprises to a successful conclusion."[5]

Contemporary Jewish perspective: "In Judaism an angel is a spiritual entity in the service of God. Angels play a prominent role in Jewish thought throughout the centuries...

"A number of numinous creatures subordinate to God appear through the Hebrew Bible; the Malach (messenger/angel) is only one variety. Others, distinguished from angels proper, include Irinim (Watchers/High Angels), Cherubim (Mighty Ones), Sarim (Princes), Seraphim (Fiery Ones), Chayyot ([Holy] Creatures), and Ofanim (Wheels). Collective terms for the full array of numina serving God include: Tzeva (Host), B'nei ha-Elohim or B'nai Elim (Sons of God), and Kedoshim (Holy Ones). They are constituted in an *Adat El*, a divine assembly (Ps. 82; Job 1). A select number of angels in the Bible (three to be precise) have names. They are Michael, Gabriel, and Satan.

"Angels can come in a wondrous variety of forms, although the Bible often neglects to give any description at all (Judg. 6:11–14; Zech. 4). They appear humanoid in most Biblical accounts (Num. 22) and as such are often indistinguishable from human beings (Gen. 18; 32:10–13; Josh. 5:13–15; Judg. 13:1–5) but they also may manifest themselves as pillars of fire and cloud, or as a fire within a bush (Exod. 3). The Psalms characterize natural phenomenon, like lightning, as God's melachim (Ps. 104:4). Other divine creatures appear to be winged parts of God's throne (Isa. 6) or of the divine chariot (Ezek. 1). The appearance of cherubim is well known enough to be artistically rendered on the Ark of the Covenant (Exod. 25). Perhaps the most ambiguous creature is the Malach Adonai, an angel that may or may not be a visible manifestation of God.

"Biblical angels fulfill a variety of functions, including conveying information to mortals, shielding, rescuing, and caring for Israelites, and smiting Israel's enemies."[6]

What a multifaceted lot God's angels are! It makes me want

to burst forth in praise for the God whose kingdom is so end-
lessly awesome.

Let the previous quotes launch us on our further discussion of
the nature of angels.

ANGELS DESCRIBED

Certainly you realize by now that most angels, if not all of
them, do *not* resemble our contemporary, cutesy Christmas
and Valentine card renditions. Far from it. They often do seem
to assume a human form, but it's not usually a feminine form
or an infantile one. Angels are *not* all blonds, and they do not
necessarily have wings. They are *much* more impressive than the
"dumbed-down" version we have ended up with.

What do they look like, sound like, act like? How can we
describe what we know about the nature of angels?

Angels are personal beings. Notice that I did not say they are
"persons." They are personal beings, and they possess:

- A personal will (1 Pet. 1:12)

- Intelligent minds (2 Sam. 14:17, 20)

- Emotional responses, such as joy (Heb. 12:22;
  Luke 15:10) and contentiousness (Jude 9; Rev. 12:7)

Angels are incorporeal and invisible. The word *incorporeal*
means "lacking in material form or substance." Angels seem to
have some sort of bodies, but not the kind you can hold on to.
Some of the Jewish scholars in the early church described angels
as having "airy" or "fiery" bodies. For the most part, they remain
invisible to our human sight.

Because their bodies are not composed of a material substance
as ours are, angels do not know what it is like to get ill, to grow
old, or to die.

Angels can appear as men. According to Matthew 1:20; Luke 1:11,
26–28; and John 20:12, angels can appear to humans, although

normally they are invisible to us. Their resemblance can be so realistic that they are at times actually taken to be human beings. (See Hebrews 13:2.)

Angels can speak to us in our own languages. The angel Gabriel, for example, had brief conversations first with the priest Zacharias (Luke 1:11) and then with Mary (Luke 1:26). Throughout this book, you will read contemporary accounts of people being spoken to by angels.

Angels have spatial limitations. Although they can move from place to place a lot more efficiently than we can, angels are not omnipresent. Only God is omnipresent. Angels seem to be in only one place at any one time, not everywhere; they are localized. They are also somewhat limited in when and how fast they can show up.

Daniel 9:21–23 describes how Gabriel engaged in "swift flight" to travel from heaven to visit him. This implies a framework of both time and space. Gabriel didn't appear to Daniel as soon as Daniel prayed. Although the angel traveled "swiftly," it took some time to get there in response to Daniel's prayer, which indicates that the angel had a great distance to travel.

Angels are powerful but not omnipotent. "Mighty ones who do his bidding"—that's what Psalm 103:20 (NIV) calls them. We read in Matthew 28:2–7 how angels rolled the giant stone away from the front of Jesus's sepulcher. (This wheel of granite would have been five to eight feet in diameter and a foot thick, and it would have weighed several thousand pounds.)

So angels are vastly more powerful than we human beings are. Nevertheless, they have much less power than God Himself does. In fact, they are totally dependent on God for their strength, and they always exercise their strength in His service.

Angels are obedient. Angels set an example for us in the way they obediently perform God's will. In essence, they help to answer the Lord's Prayer: "Thy kingdom come. Thy will be done on earth as it is in heaven" (Matt. 6:10, KJV).

Psalm 103:20 addresses the angels directly: "Bless the LORD, you His angels, mighty in strength, who perform His word, obeying the voice of His word!" (NAS).

Angels are immortal. As I mentioned previously, angels don't die. Since they were created, they have never ceased to exist. Gabriel appeared to Daniel. (See Daniel 9.) Five hundred years later, this same angel named Gabriel appeared to Zacharias and then to Mary (Luke 1). Gabriel had not grown old. This wasn't Gabriel Jr. This was the same angel both times, and he is still the same today as he was over two thousand years ago when he announced the births of John the Baptist and Jesus.

Luke alludes to the immortality of angels:

> Jesus replied, "The people of this age marry and are given in marriage. But those who are considered worthy of taking part in that age and in the resurrection from the dead will neither marry nor be given in marriage, and *they can no longer die; for they are like the angels.*"
> —LUKE 20:34–36, NIV, EMPHASIS ADDED

Just think about it. The same angels are still available today who held back the Red Sea for the children of Israel and who clogged up Pharaoh's chariot wheels. The same angel who is depicted in Ezekiel 9:3–6 as marking the foreheads of the people who would sigh and groan over the welfare of cities (in other words, the intercessors) is still putting marks on foreheads today (in other words, is still singling out intercessors for their service to God).

Do you think it was a once-in-a-lifetime assignment for those angels who proclaimed the Lord's birth in Bethlehem? Do you think they had to wait eons for that day to come, only to retire to heaven afterward? I don't think so. I think those same heavenly hosts are still actively announcing good news. Those angels are still on assignment—the very same angels, not a new generation of them.

Interesting Facts About Angels

There are several interesting facts about angels found throughout the Scriptures. These include:

- Angels need no rest (Rev. 4:8).
- Angels can be visible and invisible (Num. 22:22; Heb. 13:2).
- Angels can descend to the earth and ascend to heaven (Gen. 28:12; John 1:51).
- Angels have a language of their own (1 Cor. 13:1).
- Angels are innumerable (Heb. 12:22).
- Angels wear white garments (John 20:12).
- Angels eat food called *manna* (Ps. 78:25).
- Angels can appear in human form at times (Heb. 13:2).

—Perry Stone, *Angels on Assignment*

Fundamentals About Angels

Before we get much further, I want to make sure that I cover all the details that we know about angels. Most of us know these things already, but it's helpful to gather everything together in one place so we don't make false assumptions about the essence of angels.

Wings. Angels may or may not have wings. In the Bible (i.e., Ezek. 1:5–11 and 1 Kings 6:27), we see some angelic beings with two wings, some with four, and some with six. (Don't ask me how so many wings work aerodynamically!) We also see some angels with no wings at all, walking around like men or simply appearing out of nowhere.

Garments. Angels wear clothes, typically blindingly white ones. The white-robed angels who appeared at Jesus's tomb (Luke 24:4) are often called the resurrection angels, and I personally believe they are the same ones who appeared when Jesus ascended into heaven (Acts 1:10). But angelic clothing is not necessarily always white. When angels appear in the form of men, they wear whatever clothing is appropriate to the situation, as you can see throughout the Bible and in contemporary accounts.

Lightning. Sometimes angels are too bright for people to tell what kind of garments they wear! Jesus said that He "saw Satan as lightning fall from heaven" (Luke 10:18). Ezekiel wrote:

> As I looked, a whirlwind came out of the north, a great cloud with fire flashing forth continually, and a brightness was all around it, and in its midst something as glowing metal in the midst of the fire... They gleamed like the color of burnished bronze... The living creatures ran to and fro as the appearance of a flash of lightning.
> —Ezekiel 1:4, 7, 14

Appearance as people. Angels may look, talk, act, and dress like normal people from various cultures and ethnic origins. There are numerous reports of this. In the Bible, the accounts appear as early as the Book of Genesis, when Lot welcomed two angels with honor. But the evil men of Sodom wanted to have sexual relations with them (i.e., they really thought they were men), and they proved they were angels by the way they pulled Lot back into the safety of the house. (See Genesis 19:1–10.) The biblical passage that's most often cited with regard to angels who look like ordinary people is Hebrews 13:2: "Do not forget to entertain strangers, for thereby some have entertained angels unknowingly" ("angels unawares" in the King James Version).

Angels speak. Angels speak your language. They can speak any human language or dialect they need to speak. They also speak in a language form that is not fully known to us. (Remember the phrase "tongues of men and of angels" from 1 Corinthians 13:1.)

Sometimes angels whisper. Sometimes they speak in a normal tone of voice. Sometimes they open their mouths and shout louder than any human being could shout. They can carry on a conversation with people. Their highest joy is to broadcast the praises of God.

Angels play musical instruments. In particular, we know that they blow trumpets, which of course goes along with their role as messengers who proclaim and announce the incoming kingdom of God. (See, for example, 1 Thessalonians 4:16.) In John's apocalyptic revelation, we read, "And I saw the seven angels who stand before God, and seven trumpets were given to them...Then the seven angels who had the seven trumpets prepared themselves to sound them" (Rev. 8:2, 6).

Winds and fire. According to Hebrews 1:7, which quotes from Psalm 104:4, God "makes His angels winds, and His ministers a flame of fire" (NAS). Wind and fire are often associated with the appearance of angels.

HEAVENLY AND EARTHLY REALMS

Sometimes it seems to me that the invisible veil that separates the heavenly (eternal) realm from the earthly (temporal) realm is becoming thinner all the time. There seems to be more visiting going back and forth between the two realms than we realize.

We know that the heavenly realm will never pass away, whereas the earthly realm will, at some point, be devoured by fire. That's why planet Earth is called "temporal"; it's temporary. Where does this temporal world end and eternity begin? You can't tell, because so much of the kingdom of God is here now. We don't have to wait until we die to experience it. It's here already. That's what Jesus had in mind when He taught us to pray, "Thy kingdom come. Thy will be done, as in heaven, so in earth" (Luke 11:2, KJV). When we pray that prayer, we are asking God, as His children, to send reinforcements.

In heaven, they are waiting to come to our aid, and they pass over easily from the eternal to the temporal realm. We may not see them, but that doesn't mean they haven't come. (Or we *may* actually see them or sense their nearness, but that doesn't mean we're crazy!)

It's impossible to dissect and describe in minute detail how this works. One reason is because the kingdom of God is alive and active. Things keep shifting and changing. You can't stop it happening long enough to figure it all out any more than a biology student can pin down and dissect a healthy, living creature.

I remember a time when I was ministering in a Spirit-filled Episcopal church in Ohio. I looked out in the audience, and I could see a shining light over a particular person. I didn't know anything, but I was drawn to this person, and I started to talk. Then I paused and said nothing, because I didn't know what to say. From over on the side, I heard a word being spoken to me. No one else heard it, but I heard it as if it were an external, audible voice. I heard, "Her name is Anna." So I started talking again. I said, "You have an Anna anointing, like Anna in Luke 2. You're devoting your life to the Lord. In fact, your name *is* Anna!" She ended up falling out of her chair onto the floor, worshipping God.

Maybe that was the gift of the word of knowledge in operation, or it might have been a messenger angel right there giving me a little clip, sort of a cheat sheet from heaven. Somebody spoke and told me: "Her name is Anna." I sure felt like I had heavenly help.

ANGELS IN BENNINGTON, VERMONT

Oscar Caraballo, a pastor from Puerto Rico who lives in Vermont, has seen angels in full Technicolor. Danny Steyne of Mountain of Worship in Columbia, South Carolina, wrote this account after the Vermont School of Prayer Conference in Burlington, Vermont, in 2006. During the evening of Wednesday, June 14, 2006, Oscar began to experience a series of events, all of which involved angels and all of which involved words about the glory of the Lord being released in Vermont and the surrounding northeastern states. After an evening full of extraordinary occurrences, the following series of events began to unfold:

> "[An] Angel came to me and said wait for further instruc-
> tions from the Lord. Danny Steyne came up to me and
> said the Lord told him to tell me, 'You need to go!' The
> angel came once again and said, 'Go to Bennington,

VT, now!' It was 11:00 PM by then and the drive to Bennington was 3 hours."

Three hours later, Oscar arrived in Bennington. The Lord told him to go to the church building in the center of downtown Bennington, and not go home.

He opened the door and began to experience a phenomenal visitation of the Lord.

"I opened the door and to my surprise in the middle of the church were standing seven Angels of FIRE. To my right side was a Powerful Angel. He told me that his name is Gabriel and he introduced me to the Angels of FIRE. He told me that these were the Lord's COVENANT ANGELS. He said that power is released when they combine and work together. One of the Angels came directly toward me and he said, 'I am the one who makes things happen…' They carried the colors of the rainbow, always standing from right to left: Violet [royalty], Indigo [sovereignty], Blue [spiritual warfare], Green [growing], Yellow [mercy], Orange [worship], Red [covenant, blood of Jesus]…but they all work together…

"Each of these Angels were very innocent looking, but very powerful. They were also the most loving angels I have ever encountered. They helped you fall in love with God more and more! They had so much love in them!"[7]

These angels took Oscar on a tour of Mount Snow and the mountains around New England. He saw chariots of fire and learned what would be happening in the near future. Here are two more interesting parts of his story:

Throughout this experience, Oscar said they [the angels] were intrigued with the way we sweat. They kept saying we are made out of living water! They kept touching Oscar on the forehead when he was sweating…and they told him that they always make an effort to touch the sweat of God's children because it is so wonderful to them!!!

At one point one of the angels told him that the reason they are able to be seen now is because the rain has stopped...just like a rainbow can be seen after the rain! The earth has been saturated by the rain that has been coming for years, along with the prayers. He said they told him that Mount Snow, always covered in snow, is now saturated, and that Revival would now come in the form of a "spring of living waters coming from the earth."[8]

The last line of Danny Steyne's account sounds so much like the Lord's way of doing things: "He [Oscar] asked the Lord why he would speak to him, the Lord's response was, 'Why not?'"[9]

Why not indeed! Let's be more open to hearing from God. It seems to be our often-neglected privilege to partner with the Lord and His angels. And it's good to get to know your partners a little bit, don't you think?

THE CHARACTERISTICS OF ANGELS

By James W. Goll

*T*HE WORD *ANGEL* or *angels* is used three hundred times in the Bible, and there are one hundred four recorded angelic encounters in Scripture. That's a lot, especially considering it's only a representative sampling. The Book of Revelation records the largest number of encounters—the apostle John and others watched, listened to, or interacted with angels fifty-two times. No two of these encounters are identical.

One thing we learn from the biblical encounters is that angels are not all created equal. They were created by God to occupy certain assigned positions or "orders," if you will. Their assignments match their level of authority and status in the kingdom of God. We do well to respect this fact, even as we undoubtedly fail to comprehend or divide this reality with complete accuracy. It's not easy to define something that remains largely invisible to our earthbound eyes.

ORDERS OF ANGELS

From the early medieval church, we have inherited a more or less definite idea of the orders of angels. St. Gregory the Great, who is known as one of the doctors of the church and who died in 604, wrote about nine orders of angels:

> We know on the authority of Scripture that there are nine orders of angels, viz., Angels, Archangels, Virtues, Powers, Principalities, Dominations, Thrones, Cherubim and

31

Seraphim. That there are Angels and Archangels nearly
every page of the Bible tells us, and the books of the
Prophets talk of Cherubim and Seraphim. St. Paul, too,
writing to the Ephesians enumerates four orders when he
says: "above all Principality, and Power, and Virtue, and
Domination"; and again, writing to the Colossians he
says: "whether Thrones, or Dominations, or Principalities,
or Powers." If we now join these two lists together we
have five Orders, and adding Angels and Archangels,
Cherubim and Seraphim, we find nine Orders of Angels.[1]

St. Thomas Aquinas, also a doctor of the church (in the thir-
teenth century), described in his treatise *Summa Theologica* three
hierarchies of angels. The ranking of each hierarchy was determined based on the angels' proximity to God, and each of the
three hierarchies contained three orders of angels. St. Thomas
included the seraphim, cherubim, and thrones in the first hierarchy; the dominions, virtues, and powers in the second; and
the principalities, archangels, and angels in the third and highest
hierarchy.[2]

Archangels

Archangels stand (figuratively speaking) on the top rung of the
corporate ladder of angels. The term *archangel* indicates that they
are covering angels who are *over* other angels.

We actually know at least two of them by name—the archangels Gabriel and Michael. The word *archangel* was used specifically only one time with the name of an angel following, and
that's in Jude 9, with reference to Michael: "Yet Michael the archangel, when contending with the devil in a dispute about the
body of Moses, did not dare to pronounce upon him a railing
judgment. But he said, "The Lord rebuke you!'"

Various Christian traditions name other archangels, such as
Raphael and Uriel—and Lucifer, the original name for Satan
before he fell into rebellion against God.[3]

In Scripture, instead of the name *archangel*, we more often see the phrase "anointed cherub who covers." Consider, for example, this passage about Lucifer from Ezekiel:

> You were in Eden, the garden of God; every precious stone was your covering: the sardius, topaz, and the diamond, the beryl, the onyx, and the jasper, the sapphire, the emerald, and the carbuncle, and gold. The workmanship of your settings and sockets was in you; on the day that you were created, they were prepared.
>
> You were *the anointed cherub that covers*, and I set you there; you were upon the holy mountain of God; you walked up and down in the midst of the stones of fire. You were perfect in your ways from the day that you were created, until iniquity was found in you.
>
> By the multitude of your merchandise, you were filled with violence in your midst, and you sinned; therefore I have cast you as profane out of the mountain of God; and I have destroyed you, *O covering cherub*, from the midst of the stones of fire.
>
> —EZEKIEL 28:13–16, EMPHASIS ADDED

The term *archangel* appears in 1 Thessalonians 4:16: "For the Lord Himself will descend from heaven with a shout, with the voice of the archangel, and with the trumpet call of God. And the dead in Christ will rise first." And the names of Gabriel and Michael can be spotted throughout both the Old and New Testaments in accounts of angelic encounters such as Daniel's (Dan. 8–10; 12); Zacharias's (Luke 1:19); the visitation to Mary, the mother of Jesus (Luke 1:26); in accounts such as Revelation 12:7 ("Then war broke out in heaven. Michael and his angels fought against the dragon, and the dragon and his angels fought..."); and the ninth verse of the Book of Jude, which I quoted previously.

From time to time, people report that they have received a visitation from an archangel. In the late 1970s, a man from Boise, Idaho, named Roland Buck wrote a book called *Angels on Assignment*. In this book he told story after story of true encounters with God's heavenly messengers, including a number of encounters with the archangel Gabriel himself. I highly recommend his book.

Angel names

These three archangels—Michael, Gabriel, and the fallen Lucifer (and the handful of others, depending on your tradition)—are the only ones mentioned in Scripture by name. Do I believe *all* angels have names? That's a very interesting question. Some people believe that they do, although I don't know that we can be so sure. The book *The Heavens Opened* by Anna Rountree gives detailed descriptions of different angels. Almost every one of them told his name when he appeared.[4]

As for me, I've never had an angel come and give me his first name. I have, however, had angels come and make themselves known by a name that is a description of their tasks. I once had an angelic encounter in Knoxville, Tennessee, in which an angel announced himself as "an angel of deliverance." Is his name Deliverance? I don't know; I didn't ask! But deliverance, apparently, is his job, and I expect he's good at it. I can't count the number of times I have encountered an angel who was known as something like that.

I do believe that angels have particular areas of stewardship. Lucifer used to be the chief minister of music in heaven. (See Ezekiel 28:13, NKJV: "The workmanship of your timbrels and pipes was prepared for you [or built into you] on the day you were created.") Because he contends actively with enemy angels, Michael is often defined as a "warrior angel." (See Revelation 12 or Daniel 12.)

Some people believe that the angel who came to stir the waters at the pool of Bethesda (John 5) was the one named Raphael, whose name means "the healing of God." People say he is sent to heal the damage done by demons. We read about Raphael (as well as Uriel, both mentioned in company with Michael and Gabriel) in the Book of Enoch, which is not included in the canon of Scripture, although it is quoted from in the Book of Jude (Jude 14).[5] Raphael is one of the principal characters in the deuterocanonical Book of Tobit, and in Jewish tradition, Uriel, whose name means "fire of God," is the cherub with the fiery sword who barred the gate to Eden.

CHERUBIM AND SERAPHIM

Cherubim

Ezekiel's visions of God's throne are the greatest and most mysterious—even disturbing—visions in the Bible. Ezekiel describes the cherubim:

> Now the cherubim stood on the right side of the temple when the man went in, and the cloud filled the inner court. Then the glory of the LORD went up from the cherub and stood over the threshold of the temple. And the house was filled with the cloud, and the court was full of the brightness of the glory of the LORD. The sound of the wings of the cherubim was heard even in the outer court, like the voice of the Almighty God when He speaks...
>
> There appeared among the cherubim the form of a man's hand under their wings. Then I looked, and there were the four wheels by the cherubim, one wheel by one cherub, and another wheel by another cherub. And the appearance of the wheels was as the color of a beryl stone. As for their appearances, all four had one likeness, as if one wheel had been in the middle of a wheel. When they went, they went on their four sides. They did not turn as they went, but they followed to the place wherever the head looked. They did not turn as they went. Their whole body, and their backs, and their hands, and their wings, and the wheels that the four had were full of eyes all round. As for the wheels, they were called in my hearing the whirling wheels. Each one had four faces. The first face was the face of a cherub, the second face was the face of a man, the third the face of a lion, and the fourth the face of an eagle.
>
> —EZEKIEL 10:3–5, 8–14

The Hebrew used in this chapter is very obscure, mixing masculine and feminine forms, as well as singular and plural. Perhaps Ezekiel was trying to describe the unity and the plurality of the divine presence.

Earlier in the book he describes the cherubim as living creatures who are "fiery." They are humanoids with four hands, four wings, and four faces. One face is human, the face on the left looks like a bull's face, the face on the right looks like a lion's face, and the last face looks like the face of an eagle. "Each went straight forward. Wherever the spirit was to go, they would go and not turn as they went" (Ezek. 1:12).

How could Ezekiel describe something that is beyond words? He (and others, such as John as he was writing the Book of Revelation) did the best he could do to describe something that you would have to see yourself to believe.

Moses was instructed to portray cherubim on the ark of the covenant. The specific description is found in Exodus 25:18–22 (and is alluded to in Hebrews 9:5). The singular of cherubim is "cherub"; there were two separate ones on opposite ends of the ark, made of one piece with the mercy seat.

The Bible tells us that God "rides upon a cherub." I'd like to see that sometime! Look at Psalm 18:10: "He rode on a cherub, and flew; He flew swiftly on the wings of the wind." Also see 2 Samuel 22:11: "He rode upon a cherub as He flew, and appeared upon the wings of the wind." I guess it's only naturally supernatural for Him to do so. After all, He is "enthroned above the cherubim" (2 Sam. 6:2, NAS).

Seraphim

Like *cherubim*, the word *seraphim* is plural; the singular form is "seraph." The word means "burning one." The seraphim are described as having six wings, and they lift up a continual cry of, "Holy, holy, holy, is the Lord of Hosts; the whole earth is full of His glory" (Isa. 6:3).

Isaiah saw them "in the year that King Uzziah died," and his life was never the same again:

> In the year that King Uzziah died I saw the Lord sitting on a throne, high and lifted up, and His train filled the temple. Above it stood the seraphim. Each one had six wings. With two he covered his face, and with two he covered his feet, and with two he flew...
>
> And I said: "Woe is me! For I am undone because I am a man of unclean lips, and I dwell in the midst of a people of unclean lips. For my eyes have seen the King, the Lord of Hosts."
>
> Then one of the seraphim flew to me with a live coal which he had taken with the tongs from off the altar in his hand. And he laid it on my mouth, and said, "This has touched your lips, and your iniquity is taken away, and your sin purged."
>
> —ISAIAH 6:1–2, 5–7

Do you see the connection? The seraphim cry "holy, holy, holy" to each other all the time—and they bring purity to sinful human beings so that we can approach the throne of God. I think that when we experience the manifest presence of God and feel utterly undone and small, the seraphim have been released to come into our realm.

The seraphim aren't as hard to describe as the cherubim, but just the same, they're far outside our normal experience. Christians over the centuries have pictured their six-winged bodies differently. Daniel and Ezekiel recorded only very brief accounts, while Isaiah and John attempted to describe them in more detail. Some artists have pictured only two seraphim, one on either side of the Lord enthroned. Others have felt that there were four of them, like the four winds or four corners of the earth, and they depicted them at the four supporting corners of magnificent churches, supporting the dome of heaven. Some artists have depicted the six-winged seraphim as a cluster of wings. But some early Christians thought the wings were covering the Lord on His throne.

I need to remind you angels are incorporeal—they are spirits; they have no bodies. And yet they are described as if they do. In very important ways, our halting effort to describe such spectacular creatures does at least manage to capture certain truths about them. They are bright and fiery, purifying everything they touch. They have angelic voices, eyes, wings, hands, and feet with which to praise and serve God Almighty. Maybe someday you and I will be privileged to see them in action!

OTHER CATEGORIES OF ANGELS

Besides the archangels, the cherubim, and the seraphim, Scripture leads us to believe that there are several other possible categories of angels. I want to focus on five of them:

1. The angel of the Lord

2. Guardian angels

3. Angels assigned to churches

4. Angels of great authority

5. Strong angels

The angel of the Lord

Throughout Scripture we find occasional references to "the angel of the Lord" and "the angel of His presence." What does this mean?

> In all their affliction He was afflicted, and *the angel of His presence* saved them; in His love and in His mercy He redeemed them; and He lifted them and carried them all the days of old.
> —ISAIAH 63:9, EMPHASIS ADDED

> Indeed, I am going to send an angel before you to guard you along the way and to bring you into the place which I have prepared. Be on guard before him and obey his voice. Do not provoke him, for he will not pardon your transgressions, for *My name is in him.*
> —EXODUS 23:20–21, EMPHASIS ADDED

> And He said, "My Presence will go with you, and I will
> give you rest." Then [Moses] said to Him, "If Your Presence
> does not go with us, do not bring us up from here."
> —Exodus 33:14–15

Supernatural presences were thought to dwell within a name. Hence, an "angel of His presence" carries God's manifest presence into a place.

This is akin to "the angel of the Lord." For example, consider the familiar words of Psalm 34:7: "The angel of the LORD camps around those who fear Him, and delivers them." Also recall 1 Chronicles 21:16: "David lifted up his eyes and saw the angel of the LORD standing between earth and heaven with his sword drawn in his hand stretched out over Jerusalem. So David and the elders, covered in sackcloth, fell on their faces."

Sometimes an appearance of the angel of the Lord can be termed a *theophany,* a visible manifestation of the Lord Jesus Christ before His incarnation as a human being. The story of the fiery furnace in Daniel 3 is often cited as an example. Who was the fourth man who appeared with the three Hebrew men in the midst of the flames, who came to preserve their lives, comfort them, and demonstrate the sovereign power of God? It could have been another kind of angel, but more likely it was a preincarnate appearance of the Lord Jesus Christ. Who were the three strangers who visited Abram when he was encamped at Mamre? (See Genesis 18.) Was this Jesus in preincarnate form, accompanied by two angels?

Surely many such angelic encounters have gone unrecorded, nor are they confined to the Old Testament. Up to the present day, the angel of the Lord comes to bring *Him* into a situation. When angels of His presence show up, they usher in what we call the manifest presence of God. What they bring is "thicker" and very powerful. Some element of God Himself shows up. In comes a wave of glory, as if an angel has parted the veil. *Swoosh!* In comes a breath of the heavenly atmosphere.

Guardian angels

Some people just assume that everyone has a personal guardian angel, while others think that's only a quaint folk belief, especially since Scripture only notes the existence of such angels in two passages, both of which reflect Jewish beliefs of the time:

> Jesus called a little child to Him and set him in their midst, and said, "Truly I say to you, unless you are converted and become like little children, you will not enter the kingdom of heaven...See that you do not despise one of these little ones. For I say to you that in heaven their angels always see the face of My Father who is in heaven."
>
> —Matthew 18:2–3, 10

> As Peter knocked at the door of the porch, a servant girl named Rhoda came to answer. When she recognized Peter's voice, from joy she did not open the door, but ran in and announced that Peter was standing at the door. They said to her, "You are insane." But she insisted that it was really so. So they said, "It is his angel."
>
> —Acts 12:13–15

Experientially, I think many of us can testify to angelic protection, either on our own behalf or on the behalf of a family member or friend. I know I can.

Angels assigned to churches

In a similar way, it is likely that churches have angels assigned to them. We think of the phrase "to the angel of..." before the names of each of the seven churches in the Book of Revelation, chapters 2 and 3. Each of the seven utterances begins in the same way: "And to the angel of the church [in/of]..." Ephesus, Smyrna, Pergamum, Thyatira, Sardis, Philadelphia, and Laodicea... "write..." Specific, pointed messages of both encouragement and rebuke are given. What would the angels of these churches do with these words? Why would John be like a messenger to the angels of these churches?

Were these words addressed to actual angels, to human overseers of the churches, or to the prevailing spirit of each church—or to a combination of these possibilities? This is another case where we have more questions than answers.

Revelation 1:20, however, does state quite simply, "The seven stars are the angels of the seven churches." The Greek word *angelos* is used, from which our English word *angel* derives, and that means "messenger or courier." These particular angels are *of* the seven churches.

Angels of great authority

Angels (copied by their evil counterparts) seem to have territorial assignments. These are angels of great authority. Later in the Book of Revelation, we read:

> After this I saw another angel coming down from heaven, having great authority, and the earth was illuminated with his glory. He cried out mightily with a loud voice, saying: "'Fallen! Fallen is Babylon the Great!' She has become a dwelling place of demons, a haunt for every unclean spirit, and a haunt for every unclean and hateful bird."
>
> —REVELATION 18:1–2

Such angels of great authority perhaps rule over spheres of authority on the earth, such as cities and regions. Clement of Alexandria, an early Greek theologian, seems to have believed this was true. Referring to Daniel 10:13–21, he wrote, "The presiding powers of the angels have been distributed according to the nations and the cities."[6]

Strong angels

It may or may not be helpful to differentiate angels of great authority from "strong angels," which is another phrase used in the Book of Revelation.

And I saw a strong angel proclaiming with a loud voice, "Who is worthy to open the scroll and to break its seals?"
—Revelation 5:2

Then I saw another mighty angel coming down from heaven, clothed with a cloud and a rainbow on his head. His face was like the sun, and his feet like pillars of fire. He had a little scroll open in his hand. He set his right foot on the sea and his left foot on the land, and cried out with a loud voice, like a lion roaring. When he cried out, seven thunders sounded their voices.
—Revelation 10:1–3

Then a mighty angel took up a stone like a great millstone and threw it into the sea, saying: "With such violence shall that great city Babylon be thrown down, and shall be found no more."
—Revelation 18:21

Strong angels are *strong*! Their words carry great authority as they make declarations about heavenly decisions and major shifts.

We could say more along these lines about different types of angels, but I'll reserve that discussion for later chapters that will look at angelic assignments.

Duties of Angels

Throughout the Bible we read of the duties that are given to the angels. These include the following:

- Guarding gates (Rev. 21:12)
- Guarding the tree of life (Gen. 3:24)
- Guarding the bottomless pit (Rev. 20:1–2)
- Bringing the righteous to paradise at death (Luke 16:22)
- Executing judgment on the unrighteous (Rev. 15:1–16)

- Assisting in giving the Law to Moses
  (Heb. 2:2)
- Separating the good from the bad at
  judgment (Matt. 13:39–41)
- Gathering the elect after the Tribulation
  (Matt. 24:31)

—PERRY STONE, *Angels on Assignment*

THE COMPANY OF HEAVEN

The range and extent of the angelic realm blows your mind, doesn't it? Despite our earnest efforts to understand God's kingdom, we end up with only a partial idea of the infinite variety and unreserved power of these fellow servants of ours.

Here we have a host of superbly fashioned beings who serve Him (and, by extension, us) with an amazing combination of complete submission to a defined military ranking and complete, joyful liberty. The angels love the way God created them so much that they probably don't evaluate it—because their attention is so much on God Himself. They're eager for His next word to them, eager for their next assignment in the service of the Most Holy One.

With His help, and theirs, we can obtain a degree of the same single-hearted focus. That's my goal, until the day when I graduate to join the heavenly chorus in limitless praise and worship.

PART II

Angels in the Bible

ANGELS IN THE LIVES OF GOD'S PEOPLE

By Terry Law

*I*N BIBLICAL ACCOUNTS an angel cooked meals for a prophet, and the Israelites ate angels' food. A donkey saw an angel, and a prophet acted like a donkey—and almost got killed by an angel.

Angels fought battles for men, and a man wrestled with an angel all night. An angel saved one man from sacrificing his son of promise, and angels were present when that man's true Son of Promise was sacrificed.

An angel was involved in a jail break, and the man who escaped was mistaken for an angel. Angels brought prophetic messages about the far future, yet angels do not know the day or the hour of the Lord's return.

Four categories seem to cover most of the ways angels, mankind, and God interacted in the Bible:

1. Angels ministered to people.

2. Angels brought messages to people from God.

3. Angels helped deliver individuals in danger and nations in trouble, sometimes fighting—and winning—battles.

4. Angels administered the judgments of God.

God can send angels either to show compassion and mercy or to execute wrath and judgment. However, the reason behind all of God's actions is to forward His plans and purposes in the earth.

The best way to know that angels will be dispatched if you

should happen to need them is to cry out to God in prayer, to remain humble, and to make sure that you are fulfilling God's purpose for you. Bible teacher Norvel Hayes says the best way to "put angels to work [ministering] for you" is to obey God.[1]

There are three sure ways *not* to see a true angel of God:

1. To seek angels, not God

2. To seek beyond what has been told us in the Bible (curiosity and speculation)

3. To seek "another" way than what has been given in Scripture, as did Muhammed, the prophet of Islam, and Joseph Smith, the founder of the Mormon Church

It's important to look at the angelic visits in Scripture to give us a standard to use to judge the angelic visits of today. Angelic visits always had a purpose, and they brought people closer to God and His plan for them.

ANGELS WHO MINISTERED TO PEOPLE

Abram, patriarch of the Hebrews (whom God later renamed Abraham), had been promised a son of his own for many years. Yet Sarah, Abraham's wife, did not get pregnant.

Sarah decided to help God out by observing a custom of the time, which was to give a wife's maidservant to the husband to bear a child when the wife was unable to conceive.[2] However, when Hagar the maidservant became pregnant, Sarah was not happy. She mistreated Hagar, who ran away, apparently very discouraged. An angel appeared to Hagar at a fountain and told her to return to Sarah and that a nation would be born of the son she was carrying (Gen. 16:9–11). The angel named that son Ishmael, who did go on to have many descendants now known as Arabs.

Ishmael was fifteen when the promised son, Isaac, was born. Once again Sarah persecuted Hagar, who fled into the wilderness, this time with her son. When their water was gone, they lay down under some bushes to die. An angel again appeared to her and showed them a well of water. They remained in the wilderness near Beersheba, living off the land (Gen. 21:14–21). Even though Ishmael was not the son God promised Abraham, God still provided for his needs through the ministry of angels.

When Abraham's son Isaac needed a wife, Abraham sent his servant to find the right girl, saying, "The LORD God of heaven...shall send His angel before you" (Gen. 24:7). The servant received a supernatural sign that identified the girl (Gen. 24:10–67).

An angel actually built a fire and cooked bread for the prophet Elijah, who cried out to God for help as he fled from wicked Queen Jezebel. That food sustained him for forty days and nights (1 Kin. 19:5–8).

When Abraham's descendants came out of Egypt after spending 430 years in exile, an angel led them through the wilderness to the Promised Land (Exod. 14:19; 23:20,23; 32:34; Num. 20:16). In the wilderness, angels' food, or manna (Ps. 78:25), was provided daily for the Israelites and ministered to their nutritional needs (Exod. 16:14–18).

God also said the angel would drive out the pagan tribes from the Promised Land ahead of Israel (Exod. 33:2). However, Israel disobeyed God by making treaties with the pagans and by not pulling down and destroying all of their idols. The angel was then not allowed to help (Judg. 2:1–4).

ANGELS WHO BROUGHT MESSAGES

The first person who entertained angels "unawares" was Abraham (Heb. 13:2). Three strangers came to the door of his tent, and Abraham immediately asked them to sit down and visit for a while. Then he had Sarah and his servants prepare a meal out of their best provisions (Gen. 18:1–8).

Two of these "men" were angels and many believe the third was the Lord Himself. They delivered two important messages:

- Abraham and Sarah would at long last have the promised son, "at the set time" (a year from then).

- Judgment was to fall on the towns in the valley where Abraham's nephew Lot had chosen to live with his family.

Just before the cities were destroyed, two angels led Lot and his two daughters to safety (Gen. 19:15–22).

More than fifteen years later, at the direction of God, an angel brought a message to Abraham while he was preparing to offer up his only son as a sacrifice (Gen. 22:1–19).

Angels brought messages to Isaac's son Jacob three times. The first time, he saw angels climbing up and down a ladder into the heavens. At this place, called Bethel, the Lord confirmed that His promises to Abraham and Isaac would continue through Jacob (Gen. 28:10–15).

Later Jacob saw angels as he returned to his parents' home after twenty years of exile (Gen. 32:1–2), but at that point the visit is not explained. Years later, however, as he was dying, Jacob told his eleventh son Joseph that the "angel which redeemed me from all evil" would bless Joseph's sons (Gen. 48:16). (Was Jacob possibly referring to his guardian angel?)

The night before Jacob was to be reunited with his brother, Esau, after twenty years, an angel wrestled with him all night long. Jacob refused to let him go until he received a blessing. In the morning, the angel touched the hollow of Jacob's thigh, causing him to limp for the rest of his life. An encounter with an angelic messenger from God will change you for a lifetime (Gen. 32:24–32).

More than four hundred years later an angel appeared to Moses as a flame of fire out of a bush. It was God who spoke to Moses out of the bush and called him to lead Israel out of Egypt (Exod. 3:1–4).

A prophet named Balaam got a message from an angel that almost cost him his life. Balaam was on his way to pronounce a curse over the nation of Israel when an angel got in his way. He did not see the angel, but the donkey he was riding did. The animal tried to avoid the angel three times and finally fell down. The Lord "opened" Balaam's eyes, and he saw the problem—an angel with a drawn sword waiting in ambush (Num. 22:1–35). After that, Balaam fell down!

Angels had something to do with giving Israel the law through Moses. This is recorded in the New Testament where Stephen said in his great speech before the high priest that Israel had "received the law by the disposition of angels, but have not kept it" (Acts 7:53). Paul also said the law was "ordained through angels" (Gal. 3:19).

In the days when Israel had judges but not kings, an angel appeared to Gideon, a fearful man who was hiding from Israel's conquerors. Much to Gideon's surprise, the angel told him, "The LORD is with you, O mighty man of valor" (Judg. 6:12).

Gideon informed this visitor that his family was poor, and he was "the least" of his family. But God was calling things that were not as though they were, as He had with Abraham (Rom. 4:17). God spoke of Gideon's future potential as though it were already reality. We must learn to see ourselves as God sees us and speak of His plans for our future in faith.

Gideon finally believed the angel and led Israel to victory over Midian. He later served as one of fifteen men and women who judged Israel (Judg. 6–8). He became what the angel called him.

An angel also was involved in the life of another judge of Israel: Samson, a man known for his "might." This angel also appeared to be a man when he brought a message to Samson's mother that she was to have a child. However, she knew he was a "man of God" because his face shone like "the countenance of an angel" (Judg. 12:6). Later, he appeared to both prospective parents with instructions on how to bring up their baby to fulfill his part in God's plan (Judg. 13:2–14).

Angels delivered messages to Ezekiel, Daniel, Zechariah, and the apostle John concerning God's people and events of the end times.

In the New Testament, a Christian evangelist named Philip was in the middle of a citywide revival in Samaria when an angel told him to leave and go south. As Philip obeyed, he met an Ethiopian official who had been seeking to understand the gospel (Acts 8). That one man's salvation meant the turning of an entire nation.

An angel appeared to a Gentile army officer named Cornelius and told him to send for Peter, who would give him instructions. This officer prayed to God always and gave much alms to God's people (Acts 10).

In both of these examples, non-Christians had been sincerely seeking the Lord, and He sent an angel to be a part of the answer to their prayers.

An angel brought a message to the apostle Paul just before the catastrophic shipwreck he and other Christians underwent en route to Paul's trial in Rome (Acts 27:23–24). The angel told Paul that if he and all on board followed orders, they would be saved, although the ship and its cargo would be lost. Events unfolded just as the angel had said (Acts 27).

Angels also heralded the births of Jesus and John the Baptist, as we'll see in the next chapter.

ANGELS WHO DELIVERED PEOPLE FROM DANGER

During Israel's exile in Babylon, three young men who followed God were thrown into a fiery furnace for refusing to worship the king. To the king's amazement, however, a fourth "person" appeared in the furnace with them. The youths and their "friend" were not touched by the flames, which were so intense that those who threw them in were burned to death. The fourth figure may have been an angel or Jesus Himself (Dan. 3:19–30).

Another youth taken into exile with the other three became a prophet and a great leader of the people. Daniel experienced angelic intervention in his life several times. The first time was when he was thrown into a den of lions for refusing to worship the king (the same "crime" that got his friends in trouble earlier). This was a different king, but the outcome was the same: Daniel was untouched. He told the authorities that God had "sent his angel" and shut the lions' mouths (Dan. 6:22).

In the New Testament, the apostle Peter was delivered from prison by an angel (Acts 12). Peter was asleep when a light appeared and an angel "smote" Peter on the side and told him to get up, put on his cloak, and follow him. The chains immediately fell off his hands. At that time, "many were gathered together praying" in the home of John Mark's mother (Acts 12:12). Peter followed the angel, and when they reached the iron gate leading into the city, it opened by itself.

For years many people prayed together in the Soviet Union and the Eastern bloc, and then the "iron gate" opened by itself. I wonder how many angels were involved in that.

Judging Angelic Visits

Believers must not, and nonbelievers should not, accept anything supernatural without testing its source. Paul said to "prove all things" and to "hold fast that which is good" (1 Thess. 5:21, KJV).

John wrote: "Beloved, do not believe every spirit, but test the spirits to see whether they are from God, because many false prophets have gone out into the world" (1 John 4:1).

How do you test an angel? You do this by seeing if his visit matches those in the Bible, if his words line up with the Bible, and if the purpose that his visit achieves is biblical.

- Does he tell you he is the spirit of a dead friend or ancestor? In other words, does he draw your attention to himself or to beings other than Jesus and the Father? That is not a real angel of God. God's angels never testify of themselves.
- Does he bring you revelation that cannot be found in the Bible, say that all religions are of God, and tell you that the hereafter is a good place for everyone? That is not a real angel of God.
- Does he entertain, socialize, and hang

around after his "assignment" is over? That is not a real angel of God.

- Does he use spectacular lights, weird sounds, or odd odors to get your attention? That is not a real angel of God. When a real angel appears, he gives you a message or helps you out of danger—and then vanishes.
- Does he flatter you and build up your pride, perhaps telling you how spiritual you are? That is not an angel of God. An angelic visitation is not proof of spiritual maturity.
- Does he leave you feeling anxious, fearful, or confused? That is not an angel of God.
- Does he try to force you to do something against your inner witness? That is not an angel of God.
- Do these encounters bear spiritual fruit? Do they cause you to change for the better in some way? Or are the results harmful to you or those around you? That is not an angel of God.

If an angel tells you that you can talk to him anytime or call him in some way, or if he tells you that angels can live within you—he is a counterfeit. Real angels never become part of you, nor can you ever become an angel.

You cannot test an angel if you do not know the Bible, so dig into God's Word to discover who He is and the rich covenant we have as His children. He promises angelic protection, guidance, and deliverance as we walk humbly before Him.

—Terry Law

ANGELS WHO ADMINISTERED JUDGMENT

Almighty God also dispatches angels to carry out His judgments on nations and people whose "iniquity" is full (Gen. 15:16; 2 Thess. 2:7). God's mercy is forbearing and long-lasting. However, there comes a time when judgment can no longer be withheld, and God remains just.

Pharaoh ran head-on into God's judgment when he refused to let the Israelites go. The final and tenth plague was the angel of death passing over Egypt and killing all of the country's firstborn, both people and animals (Ps. 78:43–51).

One time an angel killed seventy thousand people because King David had counted the number of fighting men in Israel in disobedience to the Lord's command. It could have been worse, but God stopped the angel before Jerusalem was destroyed (2 Sam. 24:1–17). Sometimes innocent people suffer because those in authority disobeyed God.

Another Old Testament occasion when angels brought destruction—this time on Israel's enemies—was during the time of Elisha. At one point, Elisha and the residents of a town called Dothan were besieged by the Syrian army. Elisha may have had peace in the middle of the siege, but his servant was overcome by fear (2 Kings 6:17).

Elisha reassured him, "There are more with us than with them" (2 Kings 6:16). After Elisha prayed, his servant's eyes were opened to see horses and chariots of fire between them and the enemy.

I wonder how many Christians would see angels if their eyes were truly opened? There are more good angels with us than bad angels. At the very most, the Bible tells us, only a third of the angels followed Satan (Rev. 12:4).

The great Sennacherib, king of Assyria, got his comeuppance at the hands of an angel when he defied God by sending letters to other nations, boasting that God could not deliver Judah from his hand (2 Chron. 32:17). But God sent one angel who alone "cut off" (killed) 185,000 soldiers in the Assyrian camp (2 Chron. 32:21).

The other side of the story is that when King Hezekiah of Judah

received that threatening letter from the Assyrian king, he "went up
to the house of the LORD, and spread [the letter] before the LORD";
then he proceeded to really "lay hold" of God (Isa. 37:14–20). He
told the Lord what the Assyrians were doing to His people and
the land. After that, Hezekiah appealed to God's honor and good
name not to let the Assyrian boasts prevail.

Hezekiah did not "pray the problem," nor did he identify the
problem as his. The first words out of his mouth acknowledged
that God is sovereign Commander and Ruler over all of the earth.
According to Marilyn Hickey, Hezekiah "prayed the bigger picture."[3] The angelic intervention came in response to that prayer.

In the New Testament, Herod was smitten with disease by an
angel of the Lord because he accepted worship instead of giving
glory to God (Acts 12:20–23). He was "eaten of worms" and died.

The last time angels are shown carrying out God's judgments is
in the Book of Revelation, where angels are mentioned more often
than in any other book of the Bible. There are angels of the seven
churches in Asia, angels in heaven, angels controlling the elements, angels standing around the throne, angels blowing trumpets, angels showing visions to John, and angels overcoming the
devil and his angels. Last of all, there are the angels who bring the
plagues and disasters to earth, and there is the angel who binds
Satan and later throws Death and Hades into the lake of fire.

BIBLICAL PATTERNS

So what standards does Scripture provide for judging angelic
appearances? Here are some of the conclusions we can draw:

- Angels can come in answer to sincere prayers from
  believers and nonbelievers.

- Angels sometimes appear to be human at first,
  which is why we can be unaware of who they are.
  They often reveal their true identity before the visit
  is over.

- Angels bring messages that further God's plans on earth.

- Angelic intervention always has a purpose. Angels don't come to build relationships with humans or just socialize.

- God will withhold angelic assistance because of disobedience.

- Angels carry out God's judgments against wickedness.

Throughout this book we will look more at angels' roles in the affairs of mankind, both in Scripture and today. For now let us look at their role in what must have been the happiest time for angels: the coming of Jesus Christ.

Chapter 5

ANGELS IN THE LIFE OF JESUS

By Terry Law

HE ROAD TO Bethlehem. The road to Jerusalem. The road to Nazareth. The names of these roads are evocative of something beyond natural reality to almost everyone who has lived during the past two thousand years. As few others in history can do, their very names cause thoughts of events and people larger than our own small worlds to pop instantly into our minds.

The Great Silk Road from Italy into Cathay (China) was once a road whose very name meant romance, adventure, and treasure—but not like these three roads in what once was Palestine. These three roads denote matters beyond romance. They denote life and death, matters of eternal importance, and events that turned the world upside down.

Daily traffic on the roads to these three places that collectively could have been called the "Golden Triangle" of Palestine, the Grand Central Station of the universe, or the crossroads of the spiritual world must have been closely observed by angels, at least from the time of Abraham.

Angels did not necessarily watch because they knew in advance everything that would take place on these roads. They watched because the Lord God Himself assigned "watchers" over the land so important to His plan (Eccles. 5:6; Dan. 4:13, 17, 23).

Hal Lindsey has written that once man was created, he was watched by both angels of God and angels of light (demons posing as messengers of God).

Fantastic thought, isn't it? We believe that we can take ourselves to a remote Pacific island or an isolated mountain retreat and get away from everybody and everything. However, we are still being watched by angels. We know this from many passages in the Bible.[1]

The road to Bethlehem is where the main event in God's plan for the redemption of mankind began. The road to Nazareth is where the ministry of His Son unfolded the reality of that plan. The road to Jerusalem is where it seemed to have ended—for three days—until the grave broke open and the plan of redemption was completed.

Angels were observing or actually involved in many of the events of those thirty-three years of Jesus's life, a short lifetime that did not end on Earth but extends throughout eternity. The true reality of space with no time is something we cannot understand, but it is the home of multitudes of angels.

The noted nineteenth-century astronomer, Camille Flammarion (1842–1925), upon finally catching a glimpse of the immensity of God's universe, said:

> Then I understood that all the stars which have ever been observed in the sky...do not in the infinite represent more than a...city in a grand total of population. In this city of the limitless empire, our sun and its system represent one house—a single house among millions of habitations. Is our solar system a palace or a hovel in this great city? Probably a hovel. And the earth? The earth is a room in the solar mansion—a small dwelling, miserably small.[2]

Billy Graham pointed out that in Scripture when angels appear as angels, humans react in awe or even fear. He believes the reason is because angels represent the immensity of God and space. We are suddenly aware of how small we are compared to God and how small the earth is in relation to the universe.[3]

Somehow, our small "room in the solar mansion" has been of

central importance to the universe. God has a purpose and a plan for mankind, but we are not pawns in a divine demonstration of good triumphing over evil. God created us to have a destiny in Himself.[4]

Jesus, the only begotten Son of God, paved the way for us to live in His presence with the Father and all of the holy angels forever if we simply receive Him in our hearts and confess Him with our mouths (Rom. 10:9–10).

ANGELS AND THE BIRTH OF JESUS

Confessing Jesus with their mouths was not just "a choice" to the angels who appeared that night to shepherds watching over the flocks of their masters. Perhaps it was an assignment, but most of all it was a joy, a triumph, a privilege, and a sign that marking time on Earth was over. Time still had millennia to go before it was no more, but the time of waiting for the Redeemer, the Messiah, to be born on Earth as a child ended that night.

That night the focus of all of those angelic watchers was on a specific place: Bethlehem. Luke's Gospel gives the clearest and most lyrical account of the events on that momentous evening (Luke 2:8–14).

Imagine several shepherds huddled around a small campfire in the middle of the fields. They are wearing coats made of camel's hair for warmth, and they are huddled in the lee of a hill to get out of the wind. The Holy Land gets chilly once the sun goes down.

Some of them talk softly while others are curled up in beds they made by piling rushes in the middle of oblongs outlined by stones. It is quiet except for an occasional tinkle of a bell around a lead sheep's neck or someone's cough or the sound of a stick crackling in the fire. It's hard to imagine how quiet the night must have been at that time and in that place—no cars, no planes, no radios blaring the latest hits. When Luke wrote, "And, lo" (Luke 2:9, KJV), he was saying, "Suddenly, all at once, without any warning signal," an angel "came upon them." It must have been something like a jet breaking the sound barrier right above them.

Perhaps it was at the very moment of Jesus's birth that the skies split open in that quiet field and there was light, sound, and an unbelievable sight! The light was the glory of the Lord, the sound was celestial voices raised as one, and the sight was not just one angel but multitudes—perhaps millions! I believe all heaven was in a tumult of rejoicing and excitement at this fulfillment of God's purpose and plan.

No wonder Luke says the shepherds were "sore afraid" (Luke 2:9, KJV). That means scared-out-of-your-wits afraid or perhaps the kind of fear that results from a sudden earthquake. One angel immediately reassured them by saying, "Don't be afraid. I have good news!" (See Luke 2:10.)

The news brought by angels was the best news mankind could have had. The only news comparable for those born again will be when the sky splits open in a second, and Jesus appears for the final time. Angels will be involved in that as well, and we are told it will be just as sudden—"in the twinkling of an eye" (1 Cor. 15:52).

After the angels returned to heaven, the shepherds left their flocks and made their way into the village to find the baby who had been heralded by angels. Do you think they were so excited that they left the sheep unattended and ran off to Bethlehem? Perhaps they left one of their number to watch the sheep.

The shepherds may have been youths because younger sons usually were assigned the duty of tending the sheep. We do not know how old they were, exactly how they were dressed, or how many there were. But we can be sure of one thing: For the rest of their lives, those shepherds never forgot the angels and the baby. They never had any question about the reality of angels and probably dated everything in their lives as "before we saw the angels" or "after we saw the angels." The Bible says they went back to their sheep glorifying and praising God for the things they had heard and seen (Luke 2:20).

The shepherds then took over from the angels in telling the good news, the message of hope. The Bible says that "they made widely known the word which was told them . . . And all those who heard it marveled at what the shepherds told them" (Luke 2:17–18). In essence, they became the first evangelists.

Did you ever wonder why it was in God's plan for uneducated men of a lowly profession to see multitudes of the heavenly hosts?

Why were shepherds chosen to be the first to hear that the King of kings and Lord of lords had been born?

Was it simply because God wanted the birth of Jesus announced to commoners first and then to kings in order to reach a broad spectrum of humanity?

Was it simply that the angels were so bursting with excitement they had to tell someone to "go and see" this wonderful thing that God had done?

Was it coincidence that Jesus, born of the lineage of David in the town of David, was first worshipped by shepherds? David, His ancestor, began as a shepherd and rose to become a king.

Many questions about angels have no answers in our realm, as with other mysteries of God. What we can understand is what is spelled out for us in Scripture:

- Angels were messengers at the birth of Jesus.

- Angels ministered to Jesus after a forty-day fast.

- Angels ministered to Jesus as He prayed in the garden of Gethsemane the night He was arrested.

- Angels were there at the cross and at the grave when the stone was rolled away.

- Angels announced His resurrection and later spoke to the disciples after Jesus ascended to heaven to sit at the right hand of the Father and await the time of His return.

Angels in the Life of Jesus

Angels are not only mentioned in the Old Testament, but they were also very involved in Christ's earthly ministry:

- Angels announced the birth of Christ (Luke 1:26–38).

- An angel told Joseph to take Mary as his wife (Matt. 1:20).
- An angel warned wise men not to return to Herod (Matt. 2:12).
- An angel warned Joseph to flee to Egypt (Matt. 2:13).
- Angels ministered to Christ after His temptation (Matt. 4:11).
- An angel brought healing at the pool of Bethesda (John 5:4).
- Angels ministered to Christ in Gethsemane (Luke 22:43).
- Angels were present at the Resurrection (Luke 24:4).
- Angels announced that Christ would return again (Acts 1:10–11).

—PERRY STONE, *Angels on Assignment*

A BUSY TIME FOR ANGELS

The years of Jesus's life were a busy time for messenger angels. As the "fullness of time" drew near, the time when all things were in place and ready for the birth of Jesus, an angel was sent with a special message.

He appeared to the young girl whom God had selected as the mother of the promised Messiah. Not just any angel got this assignment, but a most important one—Gabriel. Gabriel appeared not only to Mary but also to Joseph. The man who would act as an earthly father to the Son of God needed to be told that it was all right to marry his fiancée, who was pregnant but not by him.

Even before that, Gabriel appeared to a priest officiating in the holy place. He brought this priest a message similar to that which Abraham received from God. The priest and his wife, both aged, were to have a son. This son was "Elijah," the forerunner of Jesus.

Just as an angel had named Abraham's first son Ishmael, the angel named this baby John.

Marilyn Hickey calls such "birth announcements" a part of the ministry of angels.[5] During this particular year, angels were busy bringing lots of birth announcements!

Zacharias was an ordinary priest taking his turn at executing the priest's office, but his family had been priests for generations, as was the custom. It might be understandable if uneducated shepherds had been skeptical of angels, but a priest should have known Gabriel had to be exactly who he said he was. A fallen angel, an "angel of light," would have been unable to manifest in the holy place before the veil.

You would think Zacharias would have been happy to experience a visit from an angel. However, Zacharias apparently walked by sight and not by faith. Unlike Abraham who "did not consider" the condition of his and Sarah's flesh but believed God (Rom. 4:19), Zacharias was skeptical. He was not excited, honored, or happy. Instead, Luke writes he was "troubled" and "fear fell on him."

Instead of thanking the angel for this wonderful gift from God, he said, "How shall I know this? For I am an old man and my wife well advanced in years" (Luke 1:18).

The angel replied, "I am Gabriel, who stands in the presence of God" (Luke 1:19).

The implication was, "You ought to know by seeing me here in this place that I come from the presence of God. How dare you question my word! You are doubting the Lord God Almighty, not me."

Zacharias "provoked" Gabriel, but he was only struck dumb until the baby was born. Remember Balaam? He was the prophet in the Old Testament who almost got himself killed by provoking an angel.

Can you imagine how angels must have walked through the streets of Jerusalem and watched from the heavenlies above Bethlehem, wondering how the people could be so oblivious to the great event about to burst upon them?

Did Mary and Joseph feel the presence of angels as they traveled the dusty road from Nazareth to Bethlehem when she was ready to give birth? I am sure angels hovered around them.

Did they hear the brush of angels' wings over the cave-stable—the only private place they could find? I can imagine angels surrounding the birth scene and the baby in the manger.

Angels must have been near Jesus throughout His life. However, the only other mentions we have of them before the resurrection is after He observed a forty-day fast (Matt. 4:1–11) and when He prayed in the garden of Gethsemane the night of His arrest (Luke 22:43).

The forty-day fast not only was spent without anything to eat, but it also was spent in the wilderness with wild beasts. Next a "beast" wilder than any on earth came and tempted Him. After He resisted Satan—who handled the temptation in person and then left Him "for a season"—Jesus must have been totally exhausted and very weak.

Matthew and Mark mention the angels almost as an aside, as if to say, "So, of course, angels came and ministered to Him." (See Matthew 4:11; Mark 1:13.) The word *minister* in both references is the Greek word *diakoneo*, from which we get the word *deacon*. Strong's concordance says it means "to be an attendant" or "to wait on someone."[6]

We are not told this, but the angels may have fed Jesus just as the angel fed Elijah. If the angel did not feed Jesus, he strengthened and encouraged Him in some manner. We are told that He "returned in the power of the Spirit" to Galilee and began to minister so that His fame spread throughout the region (Luke 4:14).

Jesus spoke of angels often during His ministry. He also ran across plenty of Satan's minions. The authors of *The Foundations of Pentecostal Theology* say:

> Demon-possessed people were brought to Jesus. He dealt with them as those who were possessed by casting out the demons (Matt. 8:16; 9:32–33; Mark 5:2–13).
>
> Jesus most certainly believed that He cast the demons out of those individuals. He pointed out that this fact of His ministry was part of the proof of His divine mission (Matt. 12:26–28).[7]

ANGELS AT HIS DEATH AND RESURRECTION

At the close of Jesus's three years of ministry, as time drew near for the awesome, incomprehensible conclusion of God's plan for the redemption of mankind, angels again became active in the natural.

As Jesus took the road to Jerusalem for the last time, can you see in your mind's eye the unseen legions of angels that must have hovered over Him? Perhaps they were strengthening Him for the coming ordeal.

As Jesus neared the city of Jerusalem to eat the Passover meal with His disciples, there was a "spontaneous" outburst of welcome from the throngs gathered from all over the known world for this high feast.

Is it possible that angels orchestrated this outpouring of love and welcome? (The crowd's welcome had been prophesied in Scripture.)

Were the angels shouting for joy again as Jesus was received this way? Or were they quiet, knowing what was ahead? During His arrest, Jesus remarked that, if He so prayed, His Father would give Him more than twelve legions of angels (about seventy-two thousand) for a rescue (Matt. 26:53).

As the time drew near for His trial and crucifixion, Jesus's heart was heavy and sorrowful. In Gethsemane, He left the disciples at one place and asked Peter, James, and John to pray at a place farther on. Jesus prayed alone some distance away. Instead of praying, however, Peter, James, and John did what many of us do—they fell asleep. While Jesus was waking the disciples for the second time, soldiers came to arrest Him (Matt. 26:45–46).

By being asleep, the disciples missed the opportunity to pray with Jesus, which probably caused them remorse in times to come, and they missed the visit of an angel. Luke wrote that an angel appeared to Jesus from heaven as He prayed, strengthening Him (Luke 22:43).

On the third day after the crucifixion, women came to Jesus's tomb with spices and ointments. They wondered who they could get to roll away the stone from in front of the grave, which had been carved out of the rock of a small hill. Estimates are that this "tombstone" may have weighed as much as four thousand pounds.

When they reached the grave, however, the stone was rolled away, and Jesus's body was gone! The women were quite puzzled and, I am sure, wondered if the high priest or perhaps Pilate had ordered His body taken elsewhere for some wicked reason.

Suddenly, two "men" stood before the frightened women,[8] and again, the first thing the angels said was, "Don't be afraid" (Matt. 28:1–7; Mark 16:2–7; Luke 24:1–8).

The angels asked, "Why do you seek the living among the dead? . . . Remember how He spoke to you while He was still in Galilee" (Luke 24:5–6).

At that point, Luke writes, the women "remembered his words" (Luke 24:8). They had forgotten what Jesus had told them would happen.

I wonder if angels can understand how people can forget the words of Jesus or just not believe them. Angels must shake their heads many times, thinking, "How can people do this? How can they not know that God is real, Jesus is real, and angels are real?"

After His resurrection, Jesus appeared to His disciples and other followers and spent a period of about forty days with them before He ascended into heaven. On His final day with the disciples, Jesus led them out as far as Bethany. Apparently they had no warning this was the last time they would see Him on earth. After He had talked with them a while, He was taken up into the heavens where a cloud hid Him.

At this point, we have the last message delivered by angels during Jesus's time on earth. Two "men" suddenly appeared and asked a question, as if wondering why Jesus's closest followers did not understand what was going on (Acts 1:9–11).

However, they added words of assurance that caused them to hope—words that have brought hope to His disciples throughout the ages.

Men of Galilee, why stand looking toward heaven? This
same Jesus, who was taken up from you to heaven, will
come in like manner as you saw Him go into heaven.

—Acts 1:11

As Christians, we believe Jesus will be returning for us again in
the same way that He left. What will the angels do to announce
His Second Coming?

Dick Mills wrote:

> It is my firm conviction that before the second coming
> of our Lord, there will be as much angel activity as there
> was during His first coming.[9]

That is all the more reason for us to understand what angels are,
how they are different from human beings, how they are similar,
and how they fit into God's purposes for the earth.

ANGELS AND THE NATION OF ISRAEL

By James W. Goll

 NGELS KNOW THE land of Israel better than you know your own neighborhood. They've been there for so long, they seem to have left their footprints everywhere you look. They're still patrolling the skies and the alleyways of the Holy Land, making sure that the divine will of God is accomplished. As this chapter will make clear, angels and Israel are inseparable.

We see angels throughout the history of the Jewish people, including their pre-Hebrew history contained in the pages of the Bible. We can claim this shared history, too, because our Old Testament comes directly from the Hebrew Scriptures.[1] The first mention of angels appears as early as Genesis 3, where angels were posted to guard the gates of the Garden of Eden. Then, through book after book, whether it's a prophetic message or a royal accounting of a military battle, we see angels everywhere.

We know two archangels by names that came from their Hebrew names: Gabriel and Michael. (*Gabri'el* means "man of God," and *Mikha'el* means "one who is as God.") Many of our names for the different kinds of angels come from Hebrew roots. For example, cherub (plural, *cherubim*) comes from the Hebrew *kerubh*. The phrase Yahweh *yosebh hakkerubhim* is translated into English as, "Yahweh seated upon the cherubim," and it most often refers to the design of the ark of the covenant. It can be found in 1 Samuel 4:4; 2 Samuel 6:2; Isaiah 37:16; and the first verses of the eightieth and ninety-ninth psalms.[2] It's easy to see that angels and God's chosen people, Israel, belong together.

However, what's actually important isn't Israel or angels—it's the Messiah Yeshua—the Lord Jesus Himself. He was born there. He loves the people of the entire world, but His heart is particularly focused on Israel, the land of His birth, death, resurrection, and eventual final return. It seems that, like the landowner and his servants in the story Jesus told in Luke 19:13, He has left His angels with the instruction to "occupy until I return." They are faithful to obey Him. Until the end, the angels will always be "preparing the way of the Lord." They exist to serve Him.

BIBLICAL ANGELIC ENCOUNTERS IN THE HOLY LAND

God is the same yesterday, today, and forever. And what He did before, He does again. History is His story, and He likes to weave together wonderful patterns and themes, which can show us what He may well do again in our own time.

As mentioned earlier in the book, God's angels tend to specialize. Like any specialist, they stick with the same sorts of tasks. Therefore, we can expect God and His angels to employ some of the same strategies in our day as they are on record as using in the past. To illustrate this, several examples from the history of Israel are listed in the following pages.

Gideon and the angel

There was much conflict during the period of time after the Israelites crossed into Canaan. To preserve the nation, God sent a series of leaders called judges. One of the most unlikely ones was Gideon. Here's how he found out about the assignment God had for him: "Israel was made weak before Midian and cried out to the Lord...the angel of the Lord came and sat under the oak tree in Ophrah belonging to Joash the Abiezrite. Gideon his son was threshing wheat in a winepress to hide it from the Midianites. The angel of the Lord appeared and said to him, 'The Lord is with you, O mighty man of valor'" (Judg. 6:6, 11–12).

Angel or no angel, Gideon was not convinced. These were threatening times, and he was not a noted warrior. To be sure that this messenger was from God, he asked him to wait for him to prepare an offering.

> And he said to Him, "If I have found favor in Your sight, give me a sign that it is You who are speaking with me. Please do not depart from here until I come to You and bring out my gift and set it before You."
>
> And He said, "I will stay until you return."
>
> So Gideon went and prepared a young goat and unleavened bread from an ephah of flour. He put the meat in a basket, and he put the broth in a pot, and brought them out and offered them to Him under the oak.
>
> And the angel of God said to him, "Take the meat and the unleavened bread, lay them on this rock, and pour out the broth." And so he did. The angel of the Lord reached out the tip of the staff that was in His hand and touched the meat and unleavened flatbread. Fire rose out of the rock and consumed the meat and unleavened bread. Then the angel of the Lord departed from his sight. Then Gideon perceived that it was indeed the angel of the Lord. So Gideon said, "Alas, O Lord God! I have seen the angel of the Lord face to face."
>
> —JUDGES 6:17–22

That should have been an indisputable sign, but Gideon needed a lot more convincing. So God gave him every confirmation he required, and God also gave him detailed instructions as to how to prevail over the Midianites in a strategy involving a select company of only three hundred men who would hide their torches under clay jars!

Only God could get the credit for all of this. His angel first visited Gideon as he was winnowing the harvest. (Angelic encounters, times of harvest, and times of victory all flow together.) Then, when Gideon's army blew their shofars and shattered the clay jars that hid their torches, it was a picture of how we can proclaim God's victory and let His light shine if we are unified and obedient. God is still in the same business today—the victory business.

God heard the Israelites' cry for help, and He sent an angel to notify a leader and help him muster the necessary troops, and then He helped him go to battle and win.

(An important note: we must realize that angelic involvement does not guarantee that we will be whisked away from trouble. While they do come to deliver us from our fears, they do not necessarily remove the dangerous circumstances. When they do come to help us, it is usually so that we can stand strong, fight better, and come out on top.)

Abraham and the angels

Since childhood, you've heard the story of the angelic delegation that visited Abraham and Sarah by the oaks of Mamre. "Three men," who are assumed to have been angels, arrived and spoke to Abraham. He welcomed them hospitably, and soon he discovered that they were no ordinary travelers. The spokesman declared, with the authority of God Himself, "I will certainly return to you about this time next year, and Sarah your wife will have a son" (Gen. 18:10). Then he seemed to read Sarah's thoughts and said, "Why did Sarah laugh and say, 'Shall I surely bear a child when I am old?' Is anything too difficult for the LORD? At the appointed time I will return to you, at this time next year, and Sarah will have a son" (Gen. 18:13–14).

Those angelic visitors weren't the only ones in Abraham's story. Earlier, Hagar, Sarah's maid, had had a visit from an angel when she was still pregnant with Ishmael. You will remember that the reason she was pregnant is that the still-barren Sarah (known as Sarai at the time) had given Hagar to her husband, Abraham, in hopes of achieving fulfillment of God's promise of an heir. Hagar became pregnant right away, and her relationship with her mistress deteriorated as a result, to the point that she fled. That's where the angel comes in:

The angel of the LORD found her by a spring of water in the wilderness. It was the spring on the way to Shur. And he said, "Hagar, Sarai's maid, where have you come from and where are you going?"

And she said, "I am fleeing from the presence of my mistress Sarai."

Then the angel of the LORD said to her, "Return to your mistress, and submit yourself to her authority." The angel of the Lord also said to her, "I will multiply your descendants exceedingly so that they will be too many to count."

Then the angel of the LORD said to her, "You are pregnant and will bear a son. You shall call his name Ishmael, because the LORD has heard your affliction. He will be a wild man; his hand will be against every man, and every man's hand will be against him. And he will dwell in the presence of all his brothers."

—GENESIS 16:7–12

Both angelic messages came true. Sarah did become pregnant, and she bore Isaac, just as the angel had said. Now Abraham had two sons. Sarah's relationship with Hagar did not improve, however. Eventually, when Ishmael was a young teenager, Sarah provoked Abraham to send Hagar and Ishmael away. Abraham and Sarah never saw them again, but God was looking after them, in order to fulfill His promises to Abraham—and to Hagar:

So Abraham rose up early in the morning, and took bread and a skin of water and gave it to Hagar, putting it on her shoulder, and sent her away with the child. So she departed and wandered in the Wilderness of Beersheba.

When the water in the skin was gone, she placed the child under one of the shrubs. Then she went and sat down across from him at a distance of about a bowshot, for she said to herself, "Let me not see the death of the child." She sat across from him, and lifted up her voice and wept.

And God heard the boy's voice. Then the angel of God called to Hagar out of heaven and said to her, "What is the matter with you, Hagar? Do not be afraid, for God has heard the voice of the boy where he is. Arise, pick up the boy and hold him in your hands, for I will make him a great nation."

Then God opened her eyes, and she saw a well of water. And she went and filled the skin with water and gave the boy a drink.

—Genesis 21:14–19

Israel's patriarch Abraham and his family encountered angels often. Besides the accounts above, we read about the story of Abraham's nephew Lot and the angels at Sodom. Then there's the story of Abraham's near-sacrifice of Isaac. An angel was involved in that one, too, providing the ram and instructing Abraham as to what to do:

Then they came to the place that God had told him. So Abraham built an altar there and arranged the wood; and he bound Isaac his son and laid him on the altar, on the wood. Then Abraham stretched out his hand and took the knife to slay his son. But the angel of the Lord called to him out of heaven and said, "Abraham, Abraham!"

And he said, "Here I am."

Then He said, "Do not lay your hands on the boy or do anything to him, because now I know that you fear God, seeing you have not withheld your only son from Me."

—Genesis 22:9–12

Angels guided and preserved Abraham and his family over and over again. God wanted to achieve His plan to establish His chosen people, the Jews. He also wanted to establish and bless the other people groups who arose from Abraham's seed. It's incredible to think about how it happened.

God's promises to the offspring of the patriarch Abraham,

uttered through His angels, remain valid, even though, by and large, the people of the Middle East have to this day failed to realize how much of the promise is fulfilled in Yeshua, the Lord Jesus. The Jews don't believe that He's the Messiah they have been waiting for, and the Arab world doesn't realize they even need a Savior.

That fact should compel us to our knees again and again. Jesus said, "I have other sheep who are not of this fold. I must also bring them, and they will hear My voice. There will be one flock and one shepherd" (John 10:16). We who have ourselves been "grafted in" to the vine of Israel (as Paul wrote in Romans 11) can ask God to command His angels to break through the darkness all over the Middle East.

Daniel and the archangel

The story of Daniel gives us a powerful glimpse of the invisible angelic battle in the heavenlies over this region of the world. He was, you will remember, an Israelite in exile in Babylon. He longed for the day when he and his fellow exiles would be able to return to their own land. One time, after he had been fasting and praying for three weeks, an angel appeared to him:

> In those days I, Daniel, was mourning three full weeks. I ate no tasty food, no meat or wine entered my mouth, nor did I anoint myself at all until three whole weeks were fulfilled.
>
> On the twenty-fourth day of the first month, as I was by the side of the great river which is Tigris, I lifted up my eyes and looked and saw a certain man clothed in linen, whose loins were girded with the fine gold of Uphaz. His body also was like beryl, and his face had the appearance of lightning, and his eyes were like lamps of fire, and his arms and his feet were like the gleam of polished bronze, and the sound of his words like the sound of a tumult.
>
> —Daniel 10:2–6

This angel, as we have seen in many other instances, caused great fear. The men who were with Daniel fled, even though they couldn't see the angel or hear his words. Daniel himself was overcome:

> Therefore I was left alone and saw this great vision, and there remained no strength in me, and my countenance grew deathly pale, and I retained no strength. Yet I heard the sound of his words; and while I heard the sound of his words, then I was in a deep sleep on my face with my face toward the ground.
>
> But then a hand touched me, which set me on my knees and on the palms of my hands. He said to me, "O Daniel, a man greatly beloved, understand the words that I speak to you, and stand upright, for I have been sent to you now." And when he had spoken this word to me, I stood trembling.
>
> —Daniel 10:8–11

The angel proceeded to explain what was happening and what was going to happen, and in order to do so, he had to make it possible for Daniel to withstand his powerful presence:

> Then he said to me, "Do not be afraid, Daniel. For from the first day that you set your heart to understand this and to humble yourself before your God, your words were heard, and I have come because of your words. But the prince of the kingdom of Persia withstood me for twenty-one days. So Michael, one of the chief princes, came to help me, for I had been left there with the kings of Persia. Now I have come to make you understand what shall befall your people in the latter days. For the vision is yet for many days."
>
> When he had spoken such words to me, I set my face toward the ground, and I became mute. Then one in the likeness of the sons of men touched my lips. Then I

opened my mouth and spoke and said to him who stood
before me, "O my lord, because of the vision, sorrows have
come upon me, and I have retained no strength. How can
the servant of my lord talk with you, my lord? And as for
me, there remains no strength in me now, nor is there any
breath left in me."

Then again, the one having the appearance of a man
came and touched me, and he strengthened me. He said,
"O man, greatly beloved, do not fear. Peace be unto you.
Be strong and courageous!"

When he spoke to me, I was strengthened and said,
"Let my lord speak, for you have strengthened me."

—DANIEL 10:12–19

No wonder Daniel could hardly stand to listen. This angel
was probably none other than the archangel Gabriel, and he was
explaining what the most superior of all archangels, Michael, was
going to do. (Largely because of Daniel's account, the Jews since
his time have claimed Michael as the guardian angel of Israel.)
"Then he said, "Do you understand why I have come to you? But
now I shall return to fight against the prince of Persia, and when
I have gone forth, then truly the prince of Greece will come. But I
will show you what is inscribed in the Scripture of Truth. Yet there
is no one who stands firmly with me against these forces, except
Michael your prince" (Dan. 10:20–21).

The "prince of Persia" was the evil principality who ruled over
that region. Together, Gabriel and Michael would withstand not
only that principality but also the "prince of Greece." God sent
them in response to Daniel's fervent prayers.

MODERN-DAY ANGELIC ENCOUNTERS
IN THE HOLY LAND

Angels have intervened—often openly—at every crucial juncture
in the history of Israel. We have had a chance to see this firsthand,
especially since the reestablishment in 1948 of the state of Israel.

The Six-Day War in June of 1967 was swift and successful, adding the Gaza Strip, the Sinai Peninsula, the West Bank, and the Golan Heights to the territory that Israel had already reclaimed. Then came the Yom Kippur War.

Yom Kippur War

The Yom Kippur War of 1973 could have meant the end of Israel as a state. Egypt, Jordan, Iraq, and Syria joined forces to mount a surprise attack and, they hoped, annihilate the Jews.

Lance Lambert, an English pastor and intercessor who has long been a friend of Israel, happened to be in Jerusalem when the war broke out, and he includes an account of angelic intervention in his book *Battle for Israel,* which is now out of print. In Lance's account, we can see the hand of God at work, quite literally:

> [An] Israeli captain without any religious beliefs said that at the height of the fighting on the Golan, he looked up into the sky and saw a great, grey hand pressing downwards as if it were holding something back. In my opinion that describes exactly what happened; without the intervention of God, Israel would have been doomed…
>
> The fighting became increasingly severe. Galilee was shelled and the Syrians even used Frog missiles. There were many air raids in the north but then Syria was gradually pushed back. Meanwhile, Egypt was held in the Sinai where the greatest tank battle in world history was fought on Friday, October 19th. Much of the fighting was at such close range that they weren't even able to maneuver the tanks. Jordanian radio described it as "Hell on earth."[3]

Then the prayers began to go up, although not without a struggle. Lance found that in Jerusalem, as in many places, genuine corporate prayer was becoming a lost art. So he held a school of prayer at the height of the war, and Lance and his group of intercessors saw their prayers answered—and it didn't take very long.

Their fervent prayers included prayers for world leaders, who were deciding whether and how to become involved on both sides of the war. Some Christians, who had been tutored by the late Rees Howells in crisis intercession, felt that the enemy was trying to precipitate Armageddon. Prayer was not just a good idea; it was *vital*.

Lance notes that Israel's right to exist has always been contested. Demonic powers have sought to destroy her from the very beginning of her history. This may be because, as Lance states, Israel represents spiritual realities and values. Ancient Israelites didn't leave great monuments as did the Egyptians with their pyramids, but they left us the Word of God. "In this we see her history set forth as a living, dynamic relationship with God," Lance says. "This lesson is seen both positively at the high points of her spiritual life and negatively during those times when she fell away from the Lord. God was teaching Israel that everything depends upon a right relationship to himself. It is in this way that the whole history of Israel is the setting forth of spiritual realities. It is not a matter of secular history but the unfolding of God's purpose to save mankind."[4]

I heard another testimony about what happened in the Yom Kippur War from someone who said: "In the end, there were three thousand Egyptian tanks coming up from the Sinai, and the Egyptians heard an enormous, loud, roaring sound, and they stopped their progress." The Egyptians believed that it was the sound of thousands of tanks coming against them. But there were not thousands of Israeli tanks coming. The people who gave that testimony believed that God had released His angels and that the roaring was the sound of it. Israel's troops heard the roaring sound, too. Part of that battle did not occur. It was stopped in its tracks.

God did it in the time of Abraham. He did it in the time of Gideon. He did it in the time of Daniel. And He did it at the Yom Kippur War. Angels are on assignment, and they will be released in response to the fervent cries of God's people.

The wedding of the church and Israel

I have always carried what we would call a "core value" regarding God's heart toward Israel. But I didn't teach and preach very much about the subject until I had an experience that I call "the wedding of the church and Israel." I mentioned the experience in my book *The Prophetic Intercessor*, but here I want to give you some more background about the angelic component.

When my late wife, Michal Ann, and I were beginning to travel and host some of our own conferences and seminars, we had one at a state park retreat center in Georgia. Immediately prior to this event, I had had a couple of amazing dreams in which I had watched weddings. In the dreams, I was with friends who were working to strengthen the church and who had ties with Israel. When the bride came down the aisle to meet the groom in the dreams, somehow I knew that the groom symbolized Russia and that the bride symbolized Israel. The dream had many aspects; that was just one of them. The dream was a precursor for me to go into the former Soviet Union, specifically Russia, to be part of outreaches to the Jewish people there.

Anyway, back at the retreat center in Georgia, one of the primary themes was Israel. One night, before I was supposed to speak, we were engaged in a time of worship. Suddenly, in an open vision, I saw an unusual-looking angel in the corner of the room of the lodge where we were. I had seen only a few up to that time, so I was puzzled about the clothing that this angel was wearing. The angel was wearing a brilliant white wedding gown, and I heard the angel say, "I have come to release a message on the wedding of the church and Israel."

I stepped forward to give the evening message, and all I know is that I spoke that night well beyond anything I had studied or rehearsed for. I felt as if the angel had created new faith in me and had imparted a kind of knowledge and revelation that I hadn't had before. I spoke at length about the birth of the nation of Israel, the modern-day exodus of the Jews from the lands of the north (Russia and the European countries that had been involved in the Holocaust of World War II) to Israel, and how that exodus was bringing and would continue to bring about the wedding of the church and Israel. Change is coming! It will come to both the church's perspective concerning Israel and Israel's perspective concerning the church.

You can read much more about my involvement in the outworking of the wedding of the church and Israel in chapter 9 of my book *The Prophetic Intercessor*, which is called "Israel, God's Prophetic Calendar," and in my books *Exodus Cry* and *Praying for Israel's Destiny*.

An Angel Named Israel Awakening

In renewal meetings in Long Island, New York, where I was ministering in December of 2006, I saw something that I had never seen before. During the worship portion of the closing Saturday evening service, I felt something come into the auditorium; it was as though the atmosphere had suddenly shifted. I looked up, and an angel of the Lord manifested itself flying in on the wind and hovering in the air, carrying a shofar. It was dressed in a white, flowing, radiant garment with a gold sash wrapped from one shoulder to the waist. Words were written upon the sash. The words read, "Israel Awakening." As soon as it appeared before me, its appearance departed.

I proceeded to preach my message that night on "Open Heavens and the Ministering Angels." At the close, we went into some extended ministry time. I was waiting for the proper moment to introduce this activity that I had seen during the worship time. Then, again, I felt the atmosphere shift.

At that point, I told the people that an angel named Israel Awakening had been released to bring a spiritual awakening to both the Jewish people (regarding God's purposes within Israel) and to the body of the Messiah, the church of Jesus

Christ, concerning her role of supporting Israel in the last days.

A confirmation came immediately—only God can do this. The man who was the host of the meetings then got up and read something he had scribbled on his pad of paper. He too had sensed in worship that an angel had come into the meeting that night to awaken the church to Israel. We compared our notes—both of us had written down that the name of the angel was Israel Awakening.

So get ready—change *is* coming! Angels are on assignment to both the church and to Israel.

—James W. Goll

Israel-Hezbollah conflict of 2006

In mid-July through the cease-fire in early August of 2006, news reports were dominated with the conflict between Hezbollah forces, based north of Israel in Lebanon, and the Israeli Air Force and Israeli (ground) Defense Forces.

During that time, Christians in the Western world began to intensify their prayers for Israel. Bill Yount, a prophet based in Maryland who contributed an angel story to chapter 8, had a vision:

I saw strong angels standing wing-tip to wing-tip on the borders of Israel. Momentarily, I saw a "small break" appear in a demonic black cloud that was hanging over the nation of Israel. As this small break in this cloud appeared, simultaneously the borders of Israel lit up like a flashing green light from Heaven signaling, "We've got 'a Go' for launching!"

Immediately I saw many of these strong angels being released from their duty on the borders of Israel and being sent (as in an emergency) to personally deliver messages to churches all over the world to pray for the peace of Jerusalem.[5]

Do you see how it's all tied together and how the angels play such an important role? Israel, the land of God's promise, is guarded and aided by angel battalions who are released by the prayers of faithful believers everywhere. God's eye is on Israel, and we can expect to see angels, in response to God's bidding, arise to affect events of worldwide significance.

THE HEAVENLY CITY

Think about it—the physical city of Jerusalem, the city of David, has actually given its name to the heavenly city in the highest heaven, which is thronged with the countless heavenly host:

> For you have not come [as did the Israelites in the wilderness] to a [material] mountain that can be touched, [a mountain] that is ablaze with fire, and to gloom and darkness and a raging storm, and to the blast of a trumpet and a voice whose words make the listeners beg that nothing more be said to them...
>
> But rather, you have come to Mount Zion, even to *the city of the living God, the heavenly Jerusalem, and to countless multitudes of angels in festal gathering,* and to the church (assembly) of the Firstborn who are registered [as citizens] in heaven, and to the God Who is Judge of all, and to the spirits of the righteous (the redeemed in heaven) who have been made perfect, and to Jesus, the Mediator (Go-between, Agent) of a new covenant, and to the sprinkled blood which speaks [of mercy], a better and nobler and more gracious message than the blood of Abel [which cried out for vengeance].
>
> —HEBREWS 12:18–19, 22–24, AMP, EMPHASIS ADDED

So we too join in with the heavenly choirs, worshipping and working to usher in the kingdom of God on earth, empowered by the Spirit and aided by angels, declaring, "Worthy, *worthy* is the Lamb!"

Part III

What Angels Do

Chapter 7

ANGELS WORSHIP GOD

By Ron Phillips

HEN IT COMES to what angels do, they are first and foremost worshipers of the living God! They were created to worship, as were we! Perhaps the oldest narrative in all Scripture is the Book of Job. In God's rebuke of Job, we catch a glimpse of the ancient past.

> Where were you when I laid the foundations of the earth? Declare, if you have understanding. Who has determined its measurements, if you know? Or who has stretched the line upon it? To what are its foundations fastened? Or who laid its cornerstone when the morning stars sang together, and all the sons of God shouted for joy?
> —JOB 38:4–7

Angels shouted as God the Father brought His creation into being. They were not silent observers of the great works of the Father; they responded with singing and shouting as His mighty power stretched into the vast universe.

Scripture enthusiastically accounts angels blessing and worshipping God our Father: "Bless the LORD, you His angels, who are mighty, and do His commands, and obey the voice of His word" (Ps. 103:20).

Angels are watching activities in the life of the church. First Timothy 5:21 lets us know that they will not operate when we violate what the Holy Spirit has charged us to do: "I command you

before God and the Lord Jesus Christ and the elect angels that you
observe these things without prejudice, doing nothing by partiality."

Angels Around the Throne

Since I was born again, I have had interactions with
angels. My first exposure to angels was when I had
my first trip to heaven. When I saw the Lord, He was
covered with angels.

I saw the throne, and it was covered with a myriad
of angels who were in ecstasy. They were so close
to God that they were being radiated with His love.
Their reaction to it was as if they couldn't handle
it. There was too much love. The love of God being
radiated on them was overwhelming them.

I think believers have the idea that when we are in
heaven we are going to get used to God's love, that
in eternity we will get used to being exposed to it.
No! God's love is an ever-increasing experience, and
I was seeing that even the angels themselves are
overwhelmed by it. You would think that because
these angels have been around God all this time,
since the beginning of creation, that they would be
used to it, but there are levels and levels of His love
that He reveals and releases to them.

What I saw was like an overdose, a moment
in which the angels experienced an overdose of
His love and His pleasure. The Bible says, "In Your
presence is fullness of joy; at Your right hand are
pleasures forevermore" (Ps. 16:11).

That is what I saw. I saw them in an ecstatic
experience of pleasure from the Lord.

That was my first visual encounter with angels.

And it was then that the fire of God started falling
through them onto me. It was like constant flashes
of lightning and fireballs coming out of God. He just

emanates love, so fire came on me, and that is how
I was touched by the personal fire of God—His love,
the Holy Spirit, His fire.

—GEORGIAN BANOV, EVANGELIST, COFOUNDER OF
GLOBAL CELEBRATIONS

CHURCH GATHERING AT THE END OF THE AGE

As we move toward the end of the age, angelic appearances will
become more frequent. In Hebrews, there is a biblical picture of
church gatherings that most of us have missed. I am convinced
this describes worship shortly before Jesus comes to claim the
church at the end. In our worship, the dimension of glory—the
heavenlies—breaks through and commingles with us. Could it be
that the scene described in Hebrews 12 is a picture of the church
gathered on Earth rather than heaven?

> But you have come to Mount Zion and to the city of
> the living God, the heavenly Jerusalem, and to an innu-
> merable company of angels; to the general assembly and
> church of the firstborn, who are enrolled in heaven; to
> God, the Judge of all; and to the spirits of the righteous
> ones made perfect; and to Jesus, the Mediator of a new
> covenant; and to the sprinkled blood that speaks better
> than that of Abel.
>
> —HEBREWS 12:22–24

True worship brings "the heavenly Jerusalem" to our gatherings.
We are gathering with an "innumerable company of angels."

Note the following truths. First, the church will not be afraid
of the manifest presence of God. When you read the record of
Moses in Exodus 19, essentially the Israelites were afraid of God's
presence. They had seen His mighty judgment on Egypt, and fear
took hold of them. Many people today are afraid of God's powerful, glorious presence.

So on the third day, in the morning, there was thunder
and lightning, and a thick cloud on the mountain,
and the sound of an exceedingly loud trumpet. All
the people who were in the camp trembled. Then
Moses brought the people out of the camp to meet
with God, and they stood at the foot of the mountain.
Now Mount Sinai was completely covered in smoke
because the LORD had descended upon it in fire, and
the smoke ascended like the smoke of a furnace, and
the whole mountain shook violently. When the sound
of the trumpet grew louder and louder, Moses spoke,
and God answered him with a voice.

—EXODUS 19:16–19

God came down, but the people would not draw near. Notice it
was the third day! This event was celebrated at the Feast of Pentecost.
At this encounter they received the law but missed God's presence.
They told Moses in essence, "Don't ever do this again!"

Another "third day" came fourteen hundred years later. As
prophesied, on this third day Jesus rose from the dead. At the
Feast of Pentecost, forty days later, God's power shook the earth
again. This time the Spirit's manifestations were welcomed by the
early church. Unfortunately many in the church today are afraid
of God's presence.

Look at this passage from Hebrews again and see what the
end-time church gathering should look like: "But you have come
to Mount Zion and to the city of the living God, the heavenly
Jerusalem, and to an innumerable company of angels" (Heb. 12:22).
Seven points were identified in Hebrews 12:22–27 that show us
what the end-time church gatherings will look like:

- Angels gather with the kingdom church to give
  glory to God.

- Intensified worship: Mount Zion was where David
  placed a choir and orchestra for thirty-three years,
  the length of Jesus's life on Earth. Their praise was

offered continually. When the end-time church gathers, praise and worship go to the next level.

- Innumerable angels join in the worship; in fact, there will be too many angels to count!

- Worship breaking through to the other dimension and heaven kissing the church: The separation between the spiritual realm and this world are blurred and breached in the kingdom church: "To the general assembly and church of the firstborn, who are enrolled in heaven; to God, the Judge of all; and to the spirits of the righteous ones made perfect" (Heb. 12:23).

- God speaking a fresh word about the last days through the prophetic ministry: Angelic assistance will release the prophetic word to the end-time church. The kingdom church will experience direct revelation from heaven's mercy seat. Angels will watch over that word and release it through the church: "See that you do not refuse Him who is speaking. For if they did not escape when they refused Him who spoke on earth, much less shall we escape if we turn away from Him who speaks from heaven" (Heb. 12:25).

- The church shaken to its foundations so that everything unnecessary is taken away: "His voice shook the earth, but now He has given us a promise, saying, 'Yet once more I will shake not only the earth but also heaven.' And this statement, 'Yet once more,' signifies the removal of those things that can be shaken, things that are created, so that only those things that cannot be shaken will remain" (Heb. 12:26–27).

- The church receives kingdom truth and releases kingdom power to evangelize the end-time world.

Notice that all of this happens with the presence and assistance of an "innumerable company of angels." Understand this: we should expect and embrace more angelic contact in the last days. A shaking has already begun, and angel sightings are taking place where the kingdom is breaking through.

This should not surprise us since angels are always observed near the Old Testament temple worshipping continually. Since our bodies are the temples of the Holy Spirit, our hearts become the holy of holies when we enter into intimate worship. Angels are drawn to passionate worship. When we come together in the church assembly, we should be cognizant that these glorious beings who are older than time are gathering with us. They are still giving God all their worship! What angels did at the beginning they are still practicing eons later at the end of the age. They are praising God the Father and His Son, the Lord Jesus Christ. John describes a heavenly scene in Revelation 5 where he saw and heard the voice of many angels, living creatures, and the elders worshipping around the throne. In verse 11 he indicates this massive assembly was "ten thousand times ten thousand, and thousands of thousands." They worshipped with a loud voice.

Angels Ushering in God's Presence

Have you ever been in a worship gathering where you could tell that the spiritual "temperature" went up a notch? Something seemed extra special about it. You may have identified it as what I call the "manifest presence of God."

In the natural, this happens all the time—not the manifest presence of God, but rather some natural "presence" riding into a room with a person. Even when your coworker comes back from a vacation, he or she can bring a sense of relaxation along. Or the opposite can occur: your spouse can come home from work bringing along all the tension of the difficult day. I believe that the angels, who spend so much of their time before the throne of God, can't help but bring His presence to a place! Sometimes that presence is a perceptible aroma or a feeling of electricity or a visible light. Other times it's an awe-inspiring, even weighty feeling of pressure. God's holiness supercharges the atmosphere, and that affects His angels, who can't help but bring an extra wave of His holiness wherever they go.

I remember being in Kansas City in 1975 at the National Men's Shepherds Conference, which was held in the Municipal Auditorium. A lot of the "generals of the faith" were there, most of whom have now gone on to be with the Lord. I remember Ern Baxter delivering one of the greatest messages I've ever heard, called "Thy Kingdom Come." He had an unusual degree of authority on him, and he was declaring the government of God. Something holy happened in worship, prophetic words were released, and a shift occurred. It wasn't just the generals of faith who were present—some generals of heaven showed up, too.

In response to the holy presence of God, every single man took off his shoes in a unified response of humility. We just got on our faces. It was the least we could do. None of us had crowns on our heads that we could cast before God, but we had shoes on our feet. It was a true *kairos* moment, where heaven and earth met, a holy crossroads. Angels were present, probably by the thousands, and we recognized that we were standing on holy ground. The climate shifted enormously, from one of familiarity with God to one of fear of the Lord. Angels came to the

Municipal Auditorium, carrying the golden light of
heaven to the earth.

We can assume that, whenever we feel God's
presence, angels are in a place, regardless of
whether or not we can see them. Our response is
always going to be worship—holy, holy, holy is the
Lord of hosts!

—JAMES W. GOLL

As John Paul Jackson describes the scene in his book *7 Days
Behind the Veil*, "The reason all Heaven keeps repeating, 'Holy,
holy, holy,' is not because that's just what they do up there, strum-
ming along with their little golden harps. 'Holy!' is a witness to
what God has just done. Every time God acts, the act is holy, and
so the angels and every other heavenly creature bear witness to
that holy act and cry out 'Holy!'"[1]

As allies with the angels, we cannot remain silent as we experience the mighty works of God. We too must shout His praises, for
He is worthy. If the angels, who are not recipients of the saving
grace of Jesus Christ, never stop worshipping, how much more
should we hasten to give Him all our praise!

Chapter 8

ANGELS PROTECT US

By Ron Phillips

*P*SALM 34:7 SAYS, "The angel of the Lord camps around those who fear Him, and delivers them." In Psalm 91:11 we read, "For He shall give His angels charge over you to guard you in all your ways." God's angels guard and rescue all who reverence Him. The truth of this verse was made known in the life of the late Bill Bright, head of Campus Crusade for Christ, several years ago. His travels took him from continent to continent each year. He traveled in all kinds of circumstances and often faced danger. But he says that there was always peace in his heart that the Lord was with him. He knew he was surrounded by His guardian angels to protect him.

In Pakistan, during a time of great political upheaval, he had finished a series of meetings in Lahore and was taken to the train station. Though he was unaware of what was happening, an angry crowd of thousands was marching on the station to destroy it with cocktail bombs.

The director of the railway line rushed everyone onto the train, put each one in his compartment, and told them not to open the doors under any circumstances. The train ride to Karachi would require more than twenty-four hours, which was just the time Bill Bright needed to finish rewriting his book *Come Help Change the World*.

He recounts that he put on pajamas, reclined in the berth, and began to read and write. When the train arrived in Karachi twenty-eight hours later, he discovered how guardian angels had watched over and protected them all. The train in front of them had been burned when rioting students had lain on the track and refused to move. The train ran over the students. In retaliation, the mob burned the train and killed the officials.

Bill Bright was on the next train, and the rioters were prepared to do the same for that train. God miraculously went before the train and its passengers, and there were no mishaps. They arrived in Karachi to discover that martial law had been declared and all was peaceful. A Red Cross van took them to the hotel, and there God continued to protect them. When the violence subsided, Bill Bright was able to catch a plane for Europe. The scripture is true; God does send His guardian angels to guard and rescue those who reverence Him.[1]

There are angels that desire to release the benefits of the Lord to us. These angels do not bestow the gifts and protection of God, but they desire for us to join the Lord by getting into His presence, the secret place of the Most High. Angels worship in God's presence, and there we find their favor.

In biblical times, devout Jewish men worshipping in the temple wore a covering called a *tallith* or prayer shawl. This shawl was a private covering for the intercessors—a shield to symbolize they were spending intimate time alone with God. The tallith is still worn today.

That is what our secret place is like—a covering. King David wrote, "He who dwells in the shelter of the Most High shall abide under the shadow of the Almighty" (Ps. 91:1). We are to "abide" under the shadow of the Almighty. The word *abide* means "to tarry all night." It speaks of the intimacy of a husband and wife who tarry all night loving each other. When we abide in God's presence, the divine glory covers us, loves us, and hovers protectively over us.

Having entered into this close relationship with Jesus by trust, we become the beneficiaries of divine favor and enjoy protection by the angels.

A PLACE OF PROTECTION

Like a young eagle in its mother's nest, you are safe in God's presence. His truth covers and protects you. "He shall cover you with

His feathers, and under His wings you shall find protection; His faithfulness shall be your shield and wall. You shall not be afraid of the terror by night" (Ps. 91:4–5).

Night terrors are a great problem with many today, children and adults alike. Fears of the dark remain with some youngsters well into their adult lives, yet the unknown night stalkers of hell have no right when you are in that place of protection. No arrow of the wicked can penetrate the shield of faith and trust that guards the entrance to the secret place. In His presence, the old fears leave. While others may become victims of the enemy, you will be safe because of your close relationship to God.

Some years ago, a demented man approached me after a revival service in another city. He was about to hit me in the parking lot when Eddie Adams, my staff assistant, grabbed the man's arm. With his other hand, Eddie pushed me into the car and faced my attacker for me. That night, Eddie stood between my assailant and me. He was literally my shield!

If we abide in this place of protection, then we have Jesus and His angelic hosts present to step in for us to be our shield and our protection. Read this firsthand account by Mary Beth Barnes:

> I was preparing to go through the Seven Steps to Freedom, a deliverance and counseling ministry, and I found myself very afraid of the enemy. The enemy was telling me he wasn't going to leave me alone, nor was he going to allow me to be free. I knew I had to draw close to God and give Him my fears, or else I wouldn't be free from the hold Satan had on me. As I began to pray and tell God about the fear I had inside, I really entered into His presence. This is the scripture that the Holy Spirit gave me: "Because you have made the LORD, who is my refuge, even the Most High, your dwelling place, no evil shall befall you, nor shall any plague come near your dwelling; for He shall give His angels charge over you, to keep you in all your ways" (Ps. 91:9–11).
>
> As soon as the Holy Spirit ministered this scripture to

me, I saw what seemed to be a black "glob" come out of the windows and every portal of my home; it then moved across my front yard and crossed to the other side of the road. When it was on the other side of the road it took on the shape of human-like "shadows," several dark figures.

As I continued to watch these dark figures, suddenly I saw huge figures clothed in white standing about six feet apart all the way around the property line of my home. They seemed to stand at least ten feet tall with a very broad build and held in their right hands massive flaming swords. As they stood at attention, their focus was on guarding my home and nothing more.

The black shadows tried to force themselves in between each angel but were only allowed to come as far as the angels were standing. It was as if they were hitting a piece of Plexiglas. They had absolutely no power against the authority that the angels were standing in. These angels didn't fight with them, nor did they struggle with the black shadows; they simply stood guard with the flaming swords around my "dwelling place."

On a final note, the Lord has "kept me in all my ways" and propelled me into a fearless life of freedom through the power of His Holy Spirit.

There is a place where neither devil nor disease can disturb our walk or destroy our witness for Jesus. You see, we go because of His strength! We actually carry His dwelling with us! Angels watch over our every step.

ANGELIC PROTOCOL

Angels operate on divine protocol. They are creatures of order and discipline. More often than not, we desire to skip a step and get our miracle or breakthrough instantly. But there are three important levels to climb before God will release increase. Psalm 91 gives the protocol for increase:

1. Intimacy—moving to safer ground

The first key to victory is intimacy with God: "He who dwells in the shelter of the Most High shall abide under the shadow of the Almighty. I will say of the Lord, 'He is my refuge and my fortress, my God in whom I trust'" (Ps. 91:1–2).

If you are going to avoid evil, you must have an intimate relationship with Jesus Christ. Likewise, if you desire to obey the commands of Christ, you must abide in Him. In just the first two verses of Psalm 91, we find four different names of God. Our Maker wants us to know His name, to know His very character.

How do you get into God's presence and abide there? Here is the golden gateway into God's presence: "I will say of the LORD, "He is my refuge and my fortress, my God in whom I trust'" (Ps. 91:2).

You see, God inhabits praise! When we begin to audibly confess His Word out of our mouth, when we extol His might and power, then we discover the place of intimacy with Him. You move into what the psalmist David called the secret place of the Most High, an open door to His presence.

When you look at Psalm 91:1–2, you know God desires our love! Everything flows from God when we have a passionate love for Him.

2. Invincibility—the first line of defense

This psalm moves you from intimacy to a new level of protection, I believe, provided by angels.

> Surely He shall deliver you from the snare of the hunter [translated "fowler" in the NKJV] and from the deadly pestilence. He shall cover you with His feathers, and under His wings you shall find protection; His faithfulness shall be your shield and wall. You shall not be afraid of the terror by night, nor of the arrow that flies by day; nor of the pestilence that pursues in darkness, nor of the destruction that strikes at noonday. A thousand may fall at your side and ten thousand at your right hand, but it

shall not come near you. Only with your eyes shall you
behold and see the reward of the wicked.

—PSALM 91:3–8

Once you've come to a place of complete oneness, you move
on to a place of invincibility. Psalm 91 tells us that in the safety
of the shadow of His presence we will escape many traps of the
enemy and that God will "deliver you from the snare of the
fowler" (verse 3, NKJV). In biblical times, a snare containing a
lure or bait was used to catch birds or animals. The devil sets
dangerous traps for believers, but those who are walking, talking,
and speaking forth who Jesus is will be delivered from these traps,
including traps of deception, doubt, darkness, demonic forces,
disease, disasters, and defeat.

If you are hearing from God and walking with Him on a
daily basis, it doesn't mean that disasters won't happen. It doesn't
mean the disease doesn't come; it simply means that those things
cannot deter you from Christ. Here is a guarantee of victory. Your
eyes will see as God walks you through the battlefields of life with
complete victory!

Let me share with you a story that was reported on *FOX and
Friends* news show on Christmas Day in 2008. Angels and Christmas
seem to go together. During Christmas week in 2008, Chelsea was
about to die of pneumonia. The fourteen-year-old girl was about to
be taken off life support when Dr. Teresa Sunderland saw an angelic
image at the door of the pediatric intensive care unit. The bright
white image was caught on a security camera. It couldn't have been
a strange light as there are no windows in that part of the building.
Dr. Ophelia Garmon-Brown of the hospital declares it a Christmas
miracle. By the way, Chelsea recovered immediately and came home
for Christmas.[2] Angels help in healing.

3. Immunity—the deepest level of protection

There is a difference between invincibility and immunity.
Invincibility means you can escape evil's trap. Immunity means that
long before it gets to your borders, you'll know and you will be

out of the way. Immunity means that instead of a fight, there is a place where demonic forces cannot go. God provides seasons of rest from the struggle. Notice again that the key is intimacy. Everything begins with intimate worship. The psalmist refers back to making the Lord one's dwelling: "Because you have made the LORD, who is my refuge, even the Most High, your dwelling" (Ps. 91:9).

At the place of immunity there are four things that start happening:

- *Accidents stop happening!* "No evil shall befall you" (Ps. 91:10, NKJV). All of a sudden tires do not go flat, appliances do not tear up, falls that break bones stop, and cars do not hit your car. There is a place of immunity.

- *Sicknesses stop spreading!* "Nor shall any plague come near your dwelling" (Ps. 91:10, NKJV). How would you like to get through winter without colds and flu ravaging your family?

- *Angels start helping!* Angels operate most effectively when you are intimate with the Lord Jesus. Your house becomes protected when you have made Him your dwelling! Angels will even keep you from tripping over a rock! "They shall bear you up in their hands, lest you strike your foot against a stone" (Ps. 91:12).

- *Devils start losing!* What was once over your head is now trampled under your feet! "You shall tread upon the lion and adder; the young lion and the serpent you shall trample underfoot" (Ps. 91:13). Angels will warn you and protect you from all that the enemy may try to bring against you. In many respects, it's just like a warning before a tsunami.

Millions of dollars have been spent placing tsunami-warning systems on the Indian Ocean following the devastation that hit in December 2004. These new devices are ultrasensitive, sending a split-second signal to a satellite if the ocean rises even a foot and warning affected countries within moments of detection. This reminds us of the power of our connection with God, for His warning system gives us notice and reports long before evil can come to hinder our path! His warning agents are the angels!

In the historic home of John Wesley, the great Methodist, there is a very small upstairs room. This space was his prayer room that he used daily at 4:30 a.m. No wonder so many hymns, so much ministry, and so much anointing flowed out of Wesley. He had an appointment with God at 4:30 each morning! As a result, the promise of Psalm 91:9–10 was his.

God's promise is to "set you on high" because you "set your love on Him." To be set on high indicates honor, to be made excellent, to be shown and proclaimed as special! God has made you significant and special because you love Him.

Psalm 91:14–15 reveals clear promises to those who dwell in His presence, love His name, and have no desire but to know Him better.

- *I will deliver him.* This means the enemy will never hold you in sin's spiritual prison!

- *I will set him on high.* God will take care of your reputation. Let promotion come from the Lord.

- *He shall call upon Me, and I will answer.* God will always answer your prayers.

- *I will be with him in trouble.* This promise assures you that you never will face anything alone! In Matthew 28:20, Jesus said, "Lo, I am with you always, even to the end of the age" (NKJV).

- *I will honor him.* Only the applause of heaven really matters. His "well done" is enough.

- *With long life I will satisfy him.* God will extend your days so that you will live a satisfied, full, and overflowing life and will leave this life with blazing energy across the finish line!

- *I will show him My salvation.* The word for "salvation" in this passage is *Yeshua*, which is Hebrew for Jesus! Thus, the best promise is saved for last—God will show you Jesus! To see Jesus is the beginning and end of everything.

Angels Picked Up That Car and Moved It

Many years ago my mom and dad, Charles and Frances Hunter, wrote a book on angels. It was titled, *The Angel Book,* and filled with their own experiences with angels. Angels have always been part of my family's life.

I remember the first time Mom saw an angel. It happened during a church service, and she yelled, *"Whoa!"* because the sight of him scared her. He was a really big angel, and God told her from that encounter, "This is the angel I have promised to you, to take care of you and to protect you all the days of your life."

Angelic beings are around us a lot. I think the average person today does not realize the role angels have in our lives and the effect they have on our lives. In everyday moments like driving in traffic, when something happens and suddenly you're thinking, "There's no way I could not have just hit that car!" It missed you because an angel pushed the car out of your way.

I remember one time when I was riding in a car and all of a sudden another car was coming into our lane and I instinctively yelled, "Jesus!" All of a sudden the car went back to the other lane.

One moment it was right there in our lane, and then the next it was back in the other lane. It wasn't moving back or heading toward the other lane; it was literally as if angels picked it up and moved it, and we just kept going. That's a key: when you call on Jesus, He releases the angels. It releases Him. It releases all kinds of things like that.

There was another time when I was going to a meeting. I was riding in the backseat, my daughter was in the passenger seat, and a third person was driving. All of a sudden a car was screeching toward us, coming directly toward the side of our car.

My daughter just moved her arm in a sideways motion. It was an instinctive reaction as if to push the car away. She didn't even cry, "Jesus!" She just moved her arm as if swiping the car away. And the car swerved away. It stopped heading toward us.

It was the angels who moved it. They redirected the other car, and we were saved from a crash!

How many times has God through His angels actually saved our lives? More times than we know!

—Joan Hunter, author and healing evangelist
with Joan Hunter Ministries

Something About That Name

There is just something about the name Jesus! His name is power, and within the folds of its protection, believers can know a secret place where there is anointing, safety, and blessing—a tower of strength that keeps us from evil! Our planet has become "the killing fields" of hell, yet we can live, at times, immune to all these plagues.

There is such significance in knowing God's name. This "knowing" means much more than head knowledge; it refers to the closest possible intimacy. To know God's name is to be completely broken, having learned all the secrets and nuances of His character. The name of Jesus encompasses so much! Look at a few of the names of God:

- Yahweh—the Great I Am

- Jireh—my Provider

- Tsidkenu—my Righteousness

- Rophe—my Healer

- Rohi—my Shepherd

- Nissi—my Leader and Lover

- Shalom—my Peace

- Shammah—my Companion

Yes, He is also our Christ, the Anointed One, and the Messiah of the world. He is wonderful! He is our Lord! He is before the beginning and after the end! He is the unceasing song of David resounding across time and all of creation! He is the ever-shining star that will never fade. Angels move on behalf of those who know God's names!

Christ Jesus is the One we meet in that secret place. It is His scarred hand that takes us up and His shining face that welcomes us in. There we will whisper the name of Jesus and find ourselves abiding in the Almighty, overwhelmed with the promise and blessing of His presence! And there the angels will cover us.

Chapter 9

ANGELS GUIDE US

By Ron Phillips

ANGELS MIRACULOUSLY DIRECT and protect God's people. Consider Jacob Lepard's record of an angelic direction given to a group from our church while on a mission trip in Brazil.

In June of 2005, the summer before my senior year, a group of thirteen students from our church, two parent chaperones, and our youth minister were given the opportunity to take a mission trip to Castanhal in northern Brazil. We were to be gone for ten days, spending most of our time in the city working and living with a local pastor and his family. The rest of the time we spent traveling on the Moju River, which is an offshoot of the Amazon, helping with their church-planting ministry. After we had been in Castanhal for about five days, we packed our things and boarded a bus that took us out of the city to a dock near the highway, where we met the boat that would take us up the river. We were told the area where we met the boat was considerably dangerous, as several robberies had occurred there recently. However, like nearly all threats in Brazil, it was only dangerous at night, so this time around we were safe.

Our plans for the second day out on the river were to hike from early afternoon till evening several miles into the rain forest to a village where the missionary would speak at the village church. The boat was to drop us off at the trail-head and continue down the river to meet a van that would transport the missionary, the pastor, and their families to the village. The plan was for us all to load up in the van and return to our boat by road after the church service, but we were in for a surprise. We began the hike apprehensively, having been told countless stories about the local wildlife but all the time being reassured that none of the aggressive animals came out until nightfall, long after we would arrive at the village. As the hike continued, our apprehension evolved into extreme desire to not contract a jungle parasite as our trail turned from packed dirt to rotted planks suspended above swampy wetland. Needless to say I spent far more time in the mud than on the eight-inch wide trail. This occurred for two reasons: (1) I didn't listen to my mother when she told me a foundation in gymnastics would help me later in life, and (2) the rotted planks had a tendency to bend or break under the weight of a healthy American. Regardless, right at sunset, after about two and a half hours of hiking, we emerged muddy and tired from the forest but steeped in a sense of accomplishment and respect for people who made the trip daily.

Shortly after arriving at the village we received news that the missionary, pastor, and their families had not arrived as they were supposed to, and nobody knew when they would arrive with the van. We wouldn't find out until much later that night that they had been late in meeting the van, and as a result the impatient driver had simply left. Consequently, at the exact moment that we arrived at the village, they were hitchhiking their way up the highway in a beer truck with a driver who never said a word, only smiling and giving aid when it was absolutely needed.

In looking back on that night I understand why it was so full of spiritual warfare. There are a lot of details that I could share about the service, but what moved me the most is how powerfully God moved and how unexpectedly He did it. The church was a small 30 x 30 building lit by a single light bulb connected to a car battery, and every believer from the surrounding area, probably two hundred in all, was crammed in.

In the absence of the expected missionary, our youth minister got up and spoke via translator about what was on his heart, consisting mainly of the truth of the cross and the reality of grace. At the end of the short message several people received salvation, after which nearly everyone came forward to be prayed over for healing. This last part caught all of us by surprise. I can say for sure that God was present and that He was fulfilling promises and healing His people when there were no doctors for hundreds of miles. I am astounded by what He did and the way He moved during the service. In looking back, I know that this was the reason that we were supposed to be there and the reason why we were under such heavy attack from the enemy.

By the end of the service it was well past the planned leaving time, and the others had finally been able to reach us, only to inform us that there was no van and we would have to hike back through the rain forest. The prospect of a night hike had been in the back of our minds the entire time, knowing full well that the already low chances of staying out of the mud during the day would be greatly reduced by darkness, not to mention fear of large snakes. But because we had no other option, we trusted that God would make a way. We began quoting Psalm 91 and started walking back toward the trail. Probably no more than fifty feet from the trailhead we heard somebody shouting for us to stop and go to the road instead, that there was someone waiting for us there. Not fully understanding, we walked a quarter of a mile to the deserted highway where we found an air-conditioned city transport bus waiting with the engine idling. God had made a way out, which was undeniably His doing.

We boarded the bus and found the driver sitting in the back. When we asked why he was there, his only reply was that he had been told to wait there until people arrived, never offering any more explanation than that. He drove us all the way back to the dock, where we had originally boarded the day before, in silence. There we would wait on the boat to receive word of where we were and travel downriver to pick us up. We sat together in a circle, waiting by the river and watching clouds gather overhead that signified the Amazon rainy season. All the time that we sat there in the dark, the bus driver stood alone just outside of our circle, in many ways seeming to be standing guard. As I said, we'd been told the place was very dangerous at night.

After a comparatively short wait the boat arrived, and just as the last person had gotten under the shelter of the boat, the storm hit like a tidal wave. I looked back at the riverbank and saw the bus pulling back onto the highway. I had not gotten the chance to say a word to the silent bus driver the entire night, but I've given him much thought since then. To be honest, I can't say whether he or the beer truck driver were man or angel, but I can tell the story, and I know for a fact that there was unseen opposition to the movement of God that night in the rain forest. Despite this, our God was present powerfully, faithful in fulfilling His word to believers, and, even more, was glorified. This tells me there also had to be unseen allies, and in two possible cases ones that took physical form.

The truth is no one knows who sent the bus, who paid for the bus, or why it was there. Did angels direct that bus to them? Was the driver an angel? I know our thirteen young people were protected and delivered out of the Amazon jungle by angels.

Angelic intermediaries are often used by God to get God's people from one place to another. Sometimes they simply give direction, and the believer must, by faith, obey. Such an event took place in the life of Paul when he was making his final journey to Rome. Strangely the angel could not stop the shipwreck because the sailors had already violated the laws of sailing during that season. Despite Paul's warning that the voyage would end in disaster with loss of the cargo and ship and also their lives, the captain set sail. Still Paul fasted and prayed. Soon the winds arose, the ship was battered, and when impending disaster loomed near, Paul said:

> Men, you should have listened to me and not have set sail from Crete, incurring this injury and loss. But now I advise you to take courage, for there will be no loss of life among you, but only of the ship. For there stood by me this night the angel of God to whom I belong and whom I serve, saying, "Do not be afraid, Paul. You must stand before Caesar. And, look! God has given you all those who sail with you."
>
> —ACTS 27:21–24

Because of Paul's fasting and prayer, an angel came and granted Paul the lives of all on board. Even when we make unwise decisions, angels will bring wisdom to deliver. You may be the beneficiary of the angels watching over someone else whom you have led into a mess. If you are in a storm not of your own making, cry out to God! He will send His angels to direct you.

Angelic Direction in Dreams or Visions

In Scripture, angels would at times visit through visions and dreams:

- An angel from heaven spoke to Abraham, telling him not to slay Isaac on the altar (Gen. 22:11).
- An angel blocked the path of Balaam when he was preparing to curse Israel (Num. 22:22).

- An angel appeared to Gideon to direct him in battle (Judg. 6:12).
- An angel appeared to Samson's mother, predicting the birth of a son (Judg. 13:3).
- An angel stretched his hand over Jerusalem to destroy it (2 Sam. 24:16).
- An angel strengthened the prophet Elijah (1 Kings 19:5).
- An angel shut the mouth of the lions, thus protecting Daniel (Dan. 6:22).
- An angel revealed numerous prophetic revelations to Zechariah (Zech. 1–6).

—PERRY STONE, *Angels on Assignment*

Another notable example is Lot, who, along with his family, was warned of impending judgment. It is interesting to notice the ministry of these angels to Lot. First of all, they were visible: "Now the two angels came to Sodom in the evening, and Lot was sitting at the gate of Sodom. When Lot saw them he rose up to meet them, and he bowed himself with his face toward the ground" (Gen. 19:1).

Most of us have never seen angels with our physical eyes; however, Scripture is filled with angelic appearances. In the case of Lot, not only did he see them, but he also approached them. And if this divine intersect was not dramatic enough, Lot actually invited them to his house and offered to wash their feet: "Then he said, 'Here, my lords, please turn in to your servant's house and spend the night and wash your feet; and then you may rise early and go on your way.' They said, 'No, we will stay in the open square all night'" (Gen. 19:2).

The angels wouldn't let Lot wash their feet, but they did eat the feast that he prepared: "But he strongly insisted, so they turned aside with him and entered his house. Then he made them a feast and baked unleavened bread, and they ate" (Gen. 19: 3).

They were physically attractive and looked like men.

> Before they lay down, the men of the city, the men of
> Sodom, both old and young, all the people from every
> quarter, surrounded the house. They then called to Lot
> and said to him, "Where are the men who came to you
> tonight? Bring them out to us, so that we may have rela-
> tions with them."
>
> —GENESIS 19:4–5

Sodom was a corrupt and immoral society. These angels were
not only visible but also attractive to the lost men of that city. They
did not respect the holy state of these spiritual beings. In fact, they
lusted after them. These angels also had supernatural power: "Then
they struck the men that were at the door of the house, both small
and great, with blindness so that they wore themselves out groping
for the door.... 'For we are about to destroy this place, because the
outcry against its people has grown great before the presence of the
LORD, and the LORD has sent us to destroy it'" (Gen. 19:11, 13).

These angels were there to exact judgment on the city. However,
they were subject to the needs of Lot; they served Lot: "'Hurry,
escape there, for I cannot do anything until you arrive there.'
Therefore the name of the city was called Zoar" (Gen. 19:22).

In my own life I have received direction from angels. In 1978 I
was in my eighteenth day of ministry in the village of Mingading
on the island of Mindanao, Philippines, when suddenly during the
service an earthquake caused all in attendance to flee the building.
Later that evening I could hear gunfire, and in the middle of
the night I was awakened by an English-speaking person. It was
obvious that my interpreter had fled with all his belongings, and
the soldiers assigned to protect me were nowhere to be found. The
one who awakened me said, "Get all your things together and be
ready to leave." While I packed my belongings, this stranger disappeared. As I stepped out of the bamboo hut, I saw headlights
coming up the mountain road. To my relief, it was a jeep with a
female American missionary. The same "English-speaking person"
had instructed her in the middle of the night to leave M'lang
and come to Mingading to help someone in need. I left with her

and went to the Baptist Mission Compound in M'lang. The next morning *Moros*, Muslim rebels, came to the village of Mingading looking for the American. I firmly believe an angel intervened.

Angelic Messengers

What would we do without the services of God's angelic messengers? If you sit down and start turning the pages of your Bible, you will find story after story about angels bringing messages from God. They announce forthcoming events. They pronounce God's judgments. They bring encouragement. They "direct traffic," telling people what to do, how to do it, and when to do it. Here's a quick sampling of such angelic "instant messaging," from both the Old and New Testaments:

- **Joshua 5:13–15.** Joshua encountered a commanding angel who tells him how to take Jericho: "Now it came about when Joshua was by Jericho, that he lifted up his eyes and looked, and behold, a man was standing opposite him with his sword drawn in his hand, and Joshua went to him and said to him, 'Are you for us or for our adversaries?' He said, 'No; rather I indeed come now as captain of the host of the LORD.' And Joshua fell on his face to the earth, and bowed down, and said to him, 'What has my lord to say to his servant?' The captain of the LORD's host said to Joshua, 'Remove your sandals from your feet, for the place where you are standing is holy.' And Joshua did so."
- **Judges 13:3–21.** The angel of the Lord visited Manoah and his barren wife, telling them that she would bear a son and

instructing them specifically about what to do: "Now see to it that you drink no wine or other fermented drink and that you do not eat anything unclean, because you will conceive and give birth to a son. No razor may be used on his head, because the boy is to be a Nazirite, set apart to God from birth, and he will begin the deliverance of Israel from the hands of the Philistines" (vv. 4–5, NIV). The promised baby boy was Samson.

- **Luke 1:19–20.** An archangel brought a message to Zacharias: "The angel answered and said to him, 'I am Gabriel, who stands in the presence of God, and I have been sent to speak to you and to bring you this good news. And behold, you shall be silent and unable to speak until the day when these things take place, because you did not believe my words, which will be fulfilled in their proper time.'"

- **Luke 1:28–37.** Gabriel brought a message to Mary: "And coming in, he said to her, 'Greetings, favored one! The Lord is with you…Do not be afraid, Mary; for you have found favor with God. And behold, you will conceive in your womb and bear a son, and you shall name Him Jesus. He will be great and will be called the Son of the Most High; and the Lord God will give Him the throne of His father David; and He will reign over the house of Jacob forever, and His kingdom will have no end…The Holy Spirit will come upon you, and the power of the Most High will overshadow you;

and for that reason the holy Child shall be called the Son of God. And behold, even your relative Elizabeth has also conceived a son in her old age; and she who was called barren is now in her sixth month. For nothing will be impossible with God.'"

- **Luke 2:10.** Angels filled the sky, and a spokesman-angel announced Jesus's birth to the shepherds: "Do not be afraid; for behold, I bring you good news of great joy which will be for all the people."

- **Matthew 1:20; 2:13, 19–20.** Angelic messengers spoke to Joseph in dreams to direct him to take Mary as his wife, to take Mary and the baby Jesus to Egypt for safety before Herod had all of the infants murdered, and to bring them back to Nazareth after Herod's death.

- **Matthew 28:1–7.** An angel proclaimed the resurrection of Jesus: "He is not here, for He has risen, just as He said. Come, see the place where He was lying. Go quickly and tell His disciples that He has risen from the dead; and behold, He is going ahead of you into Galilee, there you will see Him; behold, I have told you" (vv. 6–7).

—JAMES W. GOLL

Chapter 10

ANGELS STRENGTHEN US

By Ron Phillips

HREE DAYS AND nights had passed with no sleep following the birth of our second daughter. Still a seminary student, I served as a full-time pastor and was on my way to church with my head still buzzing from lack of sleep. I had scribbled an outline and a few thoughts on paper but felt exhausted and inadequate.

As I entered my small study and closed the door, a feeling of utter aloneness swept over me. With a knock on the door, Dave Davidson brought in a cup of steaming, hot coffee and a big, fresh doughnut.

"How are you, preacher?" he asked. I fell into his arms in exhaustion. Dave said, "I know you're tired, but God's angels will strengthen you!"

At exactly 11:20 that morning as I rose to preach, a warmth and strength flowed through my body and my spirit. Dave was so right! The angels came and strengthened me.

Angels are here to strengthen believers who have an intimate relationship with Jesus Christ. Angels will not do for us what we have been asked to do. They can, however, strengthen us for our assignments. Because we need the strength given us by angels, it causes us to face our own inadequacies. Often we find ourselves weary and worn out from the daily struggles of life. Fatigue is a first cousin to depression. Satan's goal is to cause us to quit! The Word of God says that in the last days Satan's emissaries will try to "wear out the saints of the most High" (Dan. 7:25, KJV). Life at its best can be a wearisome experience; however, God makes provision for our strength.

ELIJAH STRENGTHENED

The prophet Elijah had won a great victory over the forces of darkness. In the Super Bowl of spiritual warfare, Elijah had called down fire from heaven and exposed the false prophets of Baal. Elijah defeated those prophets and turned the people back to the one true God. With that battle won and the three-and-a-half-year drought broken, revival came to the land. There was no rest for the prophet, however.

Queen Jezebel made Elijah number one on her hit list and pursued him. Elijah fled until exhausted, and he sat under a "broom tree." As depression took over, Elijah wished he could die. Scripture records this marvelous story of angelic assistance as Elijah received a touch and food from an angel. In fact, the angel baked him a cake that gave him forty days of strength. (See 1 Kings 19:6–8.)

DANIEL STRENGTHENED

We find once again in Scripture the story of the prophet Daniel, who also received strength from an angel. Daniel was so overwhelmed by all God had revealed to him, he almost died. But the angel came and touched Daniel. Then the angel gave him a word from the Lord. Both the touch and the word gave Daniel strength for his assignment. (See Daniel 10:17–19.)

THE LORD JESUS STRENGTHENED

On two occasions we find our Lord receiving strength from the angels. At His temptation in the wilderness, Jesus encountered strength-sapping temptation from Satan. Remember, as we discussed earlier, Satan's goal is to "wear out" the believer. In the wilderness, Satan attacked Jesus with a threefold blow, testing His resolve. Jesus defeated Satan by answering every test with the Word of God. When the battle was over, the angels came. "Then the devil left Him, and immediately angels came and ministered to Him" (Matt. 4:11).

As our Lord faced the dreadful cup of our sins in the Garden of Gethsemane, He looked into that cup and shrank from it in horror. Yet in the end, Jesus drank its awful potion to the last dregs. How was Jesus able to face that horrible assignment? An angel came from glory to help Him: "An angel from heaven appeared to Him, strengthening Him" (Luke 22:43). Jesus Christ did not avoid the inevitable cup but was strengthened for the task by the angel.

How Believers Are Strengthened by Angels

Even in contemporary times, God's angels still come to strengthen believers during difficult times. A young man shares a story about when he had trouble recovering from surgery and an angel came to his aid:

> I required knee surgery a few years ago; I prayed a lot before surgery asking God to guide the hands of all those in the theatre and to bring me safely out of the anesthetic. I apparently inhaled too deeply the anesthetic and had a hard time coming back into consciousness.
>
> I remember being very frightened, as I did not want to die—I had so much more to live for. Immediately, a white light appeared and a voice encouraged me. It said, "Breathe, breathe, you can do it, you will come out of the anesthetic. Do not fight it."
>
> I know it was an angel of God speaking to me, so I can attest to angels being present all the time and having us always in their care. I have experienced it.
>
> Thank God for His angels![1]

Observing this story and the biblical antecedents presented in the previous section, we see some ways we may receive strength from the angels. Make note and remember the following:

- Angels strengthen those on serious assignment from God. Angels do not strengthen one simply because he or she is tired; they are available to those on kingdom assignments.

- The presence of angels releases a measure of strength. The word *appear* means to bring the assistance of one's presence. As a young boy I was threatened by a bully five years older than me. One day the bully beat me. My mother sent her younger brother with me to avenge my beating. My uncle took care of that bully! Even though I did not strike a blow, I felt strong! I was strong in my uncle's presence! When he appeared, all my weakness left. Likewise, angelic appearance routs demonic strength killers.

- Angels touch and minister to weak believers. The brush of an angel's wing can strengthen the believer for their journey.

- Angels speak the Word of God, and believers are strengthened by the word of angels. God will send us a hopeful, faithful message through the angels that will strengthen and prepare us for what lies ahead.

- Angels can cook and feed believers. With this, we see angels can use tangible items to bring strength to the body and soul of a believer, or many times angels will use people to provide the necessities that strengthen the believer.

- Angels can transport believers on occasion, as we see the deacon Philip whisked away from Samaria by an angel (Acts 8:26–40). Angels can carry us when we are too tired in our own strength and can lift us up to keep us from tripping over a stone (Ps. 91).

To summarize, angels are available to strengthen us along the way. As we see in Revelation 5:2, which speaks of a "strong angel," the word *strong* translates to mean "force, innate power." In essence, strong angels are with us to strengthen us.

An Angel at the Mall

One time I encountered an angel in human form. It happened early in my marriage, shortly before Christmas. On that particular day my husband had been, well, challenging—let's put it that way. My mother was visiting, and she and my husband and I all went to the mall. It was absolutely packed with holiday shoppers, and because of the difficulty with my husband, I was nearly in tears.

I kept telling myself, "I can't cry. I'm here with my mother, and I don't want to wreck Christmas." But I am telling you, it was very difficult.

As I stood in that crowded mall with people all around me, suddenly a man was standing right in front of me. He looked at me and said, "Things are going to get better."

When he said that, I couldn't even speak. I was frozen.

I looked away to compose myself and looked back again, but he was gone. I looked around everywhere for him because the words he spoke to me were life giving. Just those few words were encouraging and uplifting and gave me hope for the future.

I didn't realize it in that moment, but he was an angel. I entertained an angel unaware!

—LINDA BREITMAN, ORDAINED MINISTER AND
CONFERENCE SPEAKER

Chapter 11

ANGELS FIGHT FOR US

By Terry Law

I HAVE BEEN AMAZED at the recent proliferation of teachings in the church on directly attacking Satan's evil angels. It seems people have become aware that we are at war. Movements and organizations are bringing new understandings in this area to the church.

Many of these men and women have great ministries and unusual abilities at communication. They also have valid insights into the Bible and a passion to win the world for Jesus, which I admire with all of my heart.

However, I believe a basic misunderstanding about the battle between Satan's troops and the church can lead to errors and possible extremism. I could not write about angels without talking about how we can stand against evil angels and demons and cooperate with the angels of God. Conversely, I find it is necessary to write about how not to deal with them.

Although there is much truth in what spiritual warfare groups are saying, I believe that in some cases they are operating out of faulty interpretations of Scripture. The reason I am so sure of this is that I made the same mistake in my first book, *The Power of Praise and Worship*. I used the three primary scriptures that they use, and I since have seen that my interpretation was inaccurate. Those three scriptures are Ephesians 6:12, 2 Corinthians 10:3–5, and Daniel 10:12. The mistake is this: the Greek word for "strongholds" in 2 Corinthians 10:4 is *okuroma*. It appears only once in the New Testament, and I did what so many others have done: I built a major doctrine on that one word.

How many spiritual warfare choruses have been written lately about pulling down strongholds? How many "militant" choruses have been written and sung by Christians who actually are losing the real battle with Satan in their minds and flesh? How many are projecting the sin in their own hearts onto demonic forces, venting anger and hatred, yet not dealing with those things in themselves? How many cities can say they have lower crime rates because principalities and powers were "pulled down"?

I had connected those verses in 2 Corinthians 10 with Paul's outline of spiritual hierarchy in Ephesians 6:12 and used the Old Testament example of Daniel to "prove" that we should use our weapons against principalities and powers. Actually, those verses do not connect in this way, although most of the books I have read on spiritual warfare make the same artificial connection that I once did. The facts are these:

1. "Strongholds" in 2 Corinthians 10 are explained very explicitly as imaginations, high things (or thoughts) that exalt themselves above the knowledge of God. Paul wrote that we should bring every thought into obedience to Christ. Some translations are even plainer, saying arguments, theories, reasonings, speculations, or pretensions. The mind is the number-one battleground between Christians and Satan.

   These verses in no way depict a cosmic struggle against territorial spirits that rule over our cities. In fact, *none* of the verses about warfare in the New Testament really involve Christians coming against heavenly powers.

   For example, in 2 Timothy 2:3–4, the warfare in which Paul exhorts Timothy to be "a good soldier" involves the affairs of this life, not evil angels and authorities. In James 4:1–2, James calls "wars and fights" the lusts that war in your members. War for the Christian obviously refers to the war of the spirit against the flesh, as does 1 Peter 2:11. It has nothing to do with fighting evil angels or spirits.

2. Ephesians 6:12, at first glance, may seem to endorse Christians fighting against evil angels in ruling positions. "For we wrestle not against flesh and blood, but against principalities, against powers, against the rulers of the darkness of this world, against spiritual wickedness in high places" (NKJV).

   However, taken in the context of verses 10 to 18, Paul is not writing about pulling fallen angels out of the heavens but about resisting the enemy's attacks in everyday life. He is talking about the shield of faith, the helmet of salvation, the breastplate of righteousness, the sandals of peace, the sword of the Spirit, truth as a covering for the "loins," knowing the Word, and prayer (Eph. 6:13–18).

3. In Daniel 10, an angel visited Daniel in answer to his prayer and fasting. In addition to the answer Daniel sought, the angel told him that the prince of Persia had "withstood" the angel until he got help from the archangel Michael (v. 13). This verse is the foundation of most of the present teaching on "territorial spirits" and is used to explain Ephesians 6:12.

   I would like to point out that this story from Daniel took place under the old covenant. After Jesus died, rose, and ascended, there is no indication in the New Testament that territorial spirits are able to stop or hinder our prayers from getting through to God.

We are sons of God and have immediate access to the throne of grace at any time. We are told to come boldly to the throne of grace in Hebrews 10:19 because of Jesus's blood. In John 15:7, the Word says, "If you remain in Me, and My words remain in you, you will ask whatever you desire, and it shall be done for you." This obviously allows no opportunity for satanic intervention. When we understand our authority in God's kingdom, there will be no fear of territorial spirits interfering with our prayers.

Let me make it clear that I do believe there are territorial spirits, and I have encountered them in the more than eighty countries where I have traveled and ministered.

It seems clear from the Bible that Satan's evil angels are arranged in ranks of various authorities. However, I believe that Christians have not been told to pull them down. The only strongholds believers are to deal with are in their own minds, flesh, and lives. The only evil spirits we are to deal with are demons that sometimes must be cast out of people through personal ministry.

Genuine spiritual warfare mostly has to do with the mind and the flesh, which, of course, involves the influences from the world and the devil.

Genuine spiritual warfare involves fighting "the good fight of faith" (1 Tim. 6:12). That means keeping our mind renewed, our flesh in check, and resisting the temptations of the world. That is the bulk of the fighting that Christians are called to do.

To borrow a phrase from Judson Cornwall, we need to see clearly whose war this really is.

WHOSE WAR IS IT ANYWAY?

If Jesus defeated Satan, and if He "disarmed principalities and powers," then why should believers have to do that?

> And having disarmed authorities and powers, He made a
> show of them openly, triumphing over them by the cross.
> —COLOSSIANS 2:15

Since we are seated with Christ "together in the heavenly places" (Eph. 2:6), that means we already are positioned above principalities and powers. Some people are leasing airplanes to get to a high altitude and pull down "high places." Others are renting the top floors of tall buildings for this purpose.

What difference does natural altitude make? Would it have been more effective if Jesus's cross had been on Mount Everest instead of Mount Calvary?

It seems that if strongholds needed to be pulled down over cities, Scripture would give examples of the apostles doing so at such notorious locations as Ephesus, Corinth, or Rome. Kenneth Hagin Sr. wrote that instead: "Paul was busy drawing attention to Jesus. He was preaching the Word so people could come out from under Satan's control."[1]

Spiritual warfare traditionally has meant simply praying about something until the answer came. Even in the Book of Daniel, angels of God—not Daniel—fought the evil territorial spirit on Daniel's behalf. The authors of *The Foundations of Pentecostal Theology* commented:

> Nowhere are Christians told to fight the devil. Our Lord did that once for all on the cross. Our part is to claim, by faith, and stand in His victory. "Resist the devil"—do not fight him—and he is the one who will "flee from you" (James 4:7). [First] Peter 5:9 explains how this is to be done: "Whom resist, steadfast in the faith." Faith in the account of Christ's victory over the devil, and faith in God's promises, is the secret to victory… Faith in God's Word is the secret of the believer's daily triumph.[2]

So what does it mean to wrestle against things that are not flesh and blood? Vine's expository dictionary says the meaning of the Greek word *pale*, translated "wrestling," is akin to *pallo*, which means "to sway" or "to vibrate."[3] Vine wrote that this is used figuratively concerning spiritual conflict. Yet many of the proponents of territorial warfare interpret this literally and believe that we actually wrestle with territorial spirits in the heavenlies.

Paul was trying to draw a word picture for believers that opposition comes from the enemy, not from other people. The whole point he is making in Ephesians 6 is not about spiritual warfare in the heavenlies but who the enemy is. He was trying to keep Christians from fighting among themselves or even against unbelievers over things the devil stirred up.

What a wrestling match it is to dismiss past failures! What a wrestling match it is to remember that snide comments and derogatory remarks from friends or relatives do not make them our enemies! Our enemy is the one who provoked those thoughts in their minds or who reminds us of past faults and failings that have been placed under the blood of Jesus.

What a wrestling match it is to avoid self-righteousness and believe that good deeds gain us status in heaven and not to take part of the glory for what God does through us!

Spiritual Territoriality

I have no argument with those who say there are territorial spirits. My only difference is in whether or not we are to pull down foes that are already defeated.

The situation is no different with evil angels than with Satan. Few believers would slip into thinking they have to bind and pull down Satan himself. They know all they have to do is resist him in all areas of their lives. The same holds true for his angels. If Satan is a defeated foe, then so are his angels.

Satan knows his ruling spirits cannot be pulled down or bound before his "lease" runs out. Remember, his lease is not for the world, nor does it involve the kingdom of God. Satan's dominion is a time-lease on the systems that rule all areas of this planet.

We can resist him by voting in political elections as God witnesses to us through the Holy Spirit. We can cut the ground out from under Satan's ruling spirit by removing from office those people who have been in agreement with his ideas.

We can resist him in our culture by buying videos or going to movies that reflect God's ways, by buying godly books and magazines, and by watching television programs that promote the concepts of God.

We can resist him in education by becoming active on local school boards.

We can resist him by fasting and praying about any of these areas.

In other words, we can resist Satan by living a biblical, normal (as taught in the Word) Christian life.

The most important thing about that passage in Daniel is not that there are territorial spirits. It is not even that good angels fight them.

The most important thing is that God answers sincere, heartfelt prayer, even if it means dispatching angels to bring the answer. Personally, I am concerned that the devil is enjoying all this attention paid to something that he knows is wasting Christians' time and energy. In books and articles and at spiritual warfare conferences, so much time is spent focusing on Satan's power and influence that our eyes are off what Jesus already has done.

Judson Cornwall said the bigger problem with some spiritual warfare is that "the emphasis is upon the power vested in us far more than the power in the blood of Jesus Christ. It walks a very fine line between Christianity and humanism, which teaches the deity of mankind... True warfare occurs when we exalt Christ in righteousness and faith."[4]

Cornwall concludes:

> I am confident that what is going on under the title of spiritual warfare is neither spiritual nor warfare. It is fleshly activity, energized by soul power. [It] is far more mass hysteria than it is warfare. It accomplishes nothing in the heavens, and often what it accomplishes on earth is divisive, mystifying, and destructive to the participants.[5]

A Spiritual Balance

We should not back off from praying for our cities, states, and nations simply because some are operating in error or extremism. We should pray for our countries and for those in authority (2 Chron. 7:14; 1 Tim. 2:2). We should pray for people's hearts to be open to the gospel.

To live victorious lives, we must not underrate or overrate our enemy, Satan. We cannot understand how to relate either to good or to evil angels if we do not understand authority in the spirit realm.

Kenneth Hagin Sr. has described the real reason Christians cannot pull down territorial spirits over cities:

> We do not have Scripture for breaking the power of the devil over an entire city once and for all time, because a city is composed of people. People have free choice, and they can choose whom they will serve—Satan or God—and in every city many people choose to serve Satan and to continually yield to him. But we can push back the influence of darkness in prayer so that the Word has an opportunity to prevail in people's hearts and lives through the preaching of the gospel.[6]

What Hagin has said is so important, I suggest you go back and reread it. A lack of understanding concerning levels of authority is the root of the pitfalls into which some are falling in the field of spiritual warfare. That's why understanding the lines of authority in the angelic realm is relevant information for living the Christian life.

More With Us Than Against Us

As the church our job is just to believe God. We are to pray, to worship God, to declare His Word, and to unleash a torrent of angelic activity because He is ready in these last days to do everything He's ever done through history. He is ready to do it in one compact, concentrated generation. So much of what He's ready to do is going to be done with angelic partnerships, with their help, support, and activity.

We are at a time in history when the angels are with us. Even when we feel most vulnerable or weak,

God is going help us. He is going to help us come into alignment with how things really are.

Remember when Elijah's servant said to him, "What are we going do? The enemy has come for us." And Elijah prayed, "Lord, open his eyes." Elijah said to his servant, "Son, there are more with us than against us." Then the same servant, who only moments before had only seen the natural problem, discovered his eyes had been opened, and he saw hovering over the Syrian army an angelic host of warriors. That took away all his fear. (See 2 Kings 6:15–17.)

The same is true for us. Sometimes our fear is based on a lack of revelation of how things *really* are. How things really are goes like this: *God wins!*

God is great. He has released an angelic army, and the angels outnumber the demons. Angels are stronger than demons. Angels are here to help us. We are on the winning team and in the winning time.

In these last days God is going to bring such an escalation of angelic activities. It already is increasing exponentially because of the time of history we are in. It is a tremendous time for us to really be aware there are more with us than against us.

Whatever city you live in, whatever part of the world you live in, there are millions—countless numbers—of angels there. They are helping you, and they are helping God's purposes. They are bringing God's kingdom on earth and fulfilling God's business.

Don't be afraid. There are more with us than against us.

—MICHAEL MAIDEN, AUTHOR AND PASTOR OF
CHURCH FOR THE NATIONS IN PHOENIX, ARIZONA

THE AUTHORITY OF THE BELIEVER

You may be wondering, "Does the believer have authority over demons and fallen angels?" Or, "Do demons and fallen angels retain any authority over people?" The answer to these questions is found when believers realize the authority delegated to them through the finished work of Christ. Author Neil Anderson wrote in his book *Victory Over the Darkness*:

> When you don't understand the doctrinal truths pertaining to your position in Christ, you have no ground for success in the practical arena. How can you hope to stand firm against the schemes of the devil (Eph. 6:11), if you have not internalized that you are already victoriously raised up with Him and seated with Him in the heavenly places in Christ Jesus?[7]

If we are seated with Christ as Ephesians 2:6 says, then our position is far above all principalities and powers of darkness. Kenneth Hagin Sr., wrote: "Our position as the church is a position of authority, honor, and triumph—not failure, depression, and defeat."[8]

The truth of the authority of the believer has everything to do with authority in the angelic world. Our knowledge of authority affects both the good and bad angels. Both respond to authority. They understand authority, which many human beings do not. The biggest problem with the church is that we have never fully realized the finished work of Christ and how it relates directly to us.

When we understand that we already have authority over principalities and powers, we do not try to "pull them down" as if we still had to gain the ascendancy. When we understand that we already have authority, we do not go to battle against the territorial spirits over our area. When we fight to take authority over Satan, we are attributing to him authority he does not have.

Why are the hosts of darkness ruling in so many countries, then? They rule because the systems of those countries are Satan's territories and believers are not walking in enough light to transform those territories through the Great Commission (Mark 16:15–18).

Why are the powers of darkness ruling in so many believers' lives? They rule because believers are not exercising the authority of Jesus, even if they know they have it.

We need to understand, however, that our authority in Christ gives us no authority over another person's will and right to choose. Even Jesus does not exercise His authority to make everyone get saved.

AUTHORITY AMONG FALLEN ANGELS AND DEMONS

What is authority anyway? What does it mean to be *in authority*? It means to rule something, "to be in charge." Some people confuse *authority* and *power*. Authority is the right to rule; power is the strength or force involved in enforcing authority.

In the heavenly realm, both good and evil angels operate without exception along lines of authority. I believe it helps to know what kind of a territorial spirit is over certain areas, because you can then find the right scriptures to preach or pray against its thought systems. Where I differ with recent spiritual warfare teachings is with the strategies being taught and the doctrine behind the strategies.

"Spiritual mapping" is a teaching that suggests studying the history and social patterns of areas to find what evil spirit is in charge of their spiritual systems. Why are some areas more oppressive, more idolatrous, more spiritually barren than others? George Otis Jr. asks these good questions:

> Why, for instance, has Mesopotamia put out such a long string of tyrannical rulers?
>
> Why is the nation of Haiti the premiere social and economic eyesore in the Western Hemisphere?
>
> Why do the Andean nations of South America [especially Colombia] always seem to rank near the top of the world's annual per capita homicide statistics?

Why is there so much overt demonic activity in and
around the Himalayan Mountains?

Why has Japan been such a hard nut to crack with
the gospel?[9]

Spiritual territoriality has a great deal to do with the way things
are in any part of the world. In my many years of ministering in
the Soviet world, I have been able to identify various spiritual
powers over geographical areas.

In 1980, I was attending a charismatic leadership conference
near St. Louis. Fifty or sixty men had gathered to discuss what
God was doing in the world. In the middle of the conference, a
Roman Catholic lay leader walked in with the news that Pope
John Paul had been shot.

The speaker immediately suggested we get on our knees and
pray. As I began to intercede, a spiritual darkness came over me.
I knew a territorial spirit was behind the attack on the pope's
life, and I recognized that spirit because I had dealt with it in
the Soviet Union. I suspected the intelligence agency, the KGB,
had something to do with the attack. (I was familiar with them
because they had interrogated me five times.)

I said as much to the group. However, the next day the news
reports said the man who shot the pope was a right-wing Muslim
fundamentalist from Turkey. I am sure that it appeared as if my
conclusions were wrong. I left it at that because I couldn't prove
a subjective recognition of a spirit. About a year and a half later,
though, the truth was revealed by the Mossad, Israel's intelligence
service, that the pope's assassin actually had been trained by the
KGB in Bulgaria.

There is no question in my mind that there are territorial spirits
because the evidence of their activity is so apparent. However,
one might ask this question: If the church has authority over evil
powers, why are they still operating?

- Satan and his evil angels will operate until Adam's
  lease runs out.

- The believer has a lack of knowledge (Hosea 4:6).

- Sin in someone's life opens the door for oppression.

- A missing "shield of faith" lets fiery darts slip through (Eph. 6:16).

- An evil angel or demon cons someone into accepting it as an angel and receiving its thoughts and doctrines. This is happening right now across the United States and other countries through books, films, and videos about "angels."

However, the bottom line of all these questions is that God is in charge. Jesus has delegated all power and authority in heaven and earth to the church. Believers have authority over all the power of the enemy as they carry out Jesus's commission in Mark 16:15–18 to evangelize the world.

Angels Will Fight Against Your Enemies

The writer of Psalm 35 requested God to deliver him from those who persecuted him. While persecution is guaranteed in the life of a true believer, God will not allow the enemies of the faith to continue in their opposition against the gospel without His supernatural intervention.

The psalmist requested: "Let them be like chaff before the wind, and let the angel of the LORD chase them. Let their way be dark and slippery, and let the angel of the LORD pursue them" (Ps. 35:5–6).

One of our personal friends and ministry missionaries, Kelvin McDaniel, has experienced God's protective hedge firsthand on numerous occasions. After returning from Indonesia several years ago, he shared this remarkable, firsthand account of God's angelic intervention on behalf of a church located in the midst of the largest Islamic population in the world. I quote from a letter sent to my office from missionary McDaniel:

> After years of terrorism against Christians in Indonesia, many of the wooden church structures have been burned down in the remote areas and islands. During a mission trip to Indonesia, I was asked by two dear Indonesian believers to preach at a remote church in West Java, which was one of the only wooden churches still standing, as every burnable structure (churches) within a one-hundred-mile radius had been burned to the ground.
>
> After arriving on a Monday night, the small, white, wooden building, which could only hold two hundred people, was entirely packed. Giant speakers were set outside so the message could be heard in the Muslim communities over a mile in all directions. After the service, where souls were won to Christ, we piled in the vehicle and drove back to the city. At approximately five o'clock on Tuesday, after arriving at the airport, the translator's cell phone rang, and there was a desperate plea from the pastor of the small wooden church to speak with me to relate an astonishing event that had occurred.
>
> That morning, a flatbed truck filled with Islamic terrorists arrived at the front door of the church. The pastor and his family live next door in a three-room apartment. The men began dragging a fifty-five-gallon oil drum filled with fuel, pouring it on the steps, and kicking in the door to pour it into the small church sanctuary. The fuel covered the floor, and the smell of gas filled the building. The pastor's wife ran out screaming for them not to burn the building down. She told them her children were in the apartment and this was the

house of God. She then fell to her knees in the mixture of fuel, mud, and sod, begging them not to burn the house of God.

The fanatics began yelling that they were doing God's work by burning down the deceitful church. The leader slammed the now-empty barrel over the top of the stairs and into the building. The pastor's wife began pleading in prayer for the hand of the Lord to be with her and the family and the church building.

As the truck and the men pulled away to be out of danger's way, a lone man pulled out a box of matches. As he attempted to strike the match across the side of the box, nothing happened. He fumbled through the box, pulling out another match, only to have the same results. By this time hundreds had gathered to see the outcome of this assault on the Christian church. After several attempts, he suddenly shrieked out a terrible, blood-curdling scream and began running with his face frozen in a look of fear. He was grabbing his head and screaming with such passionate horror it seemed his mind had snapped.

Eventually, someone tackled him to prevent him from injuring himself and to assess his problem. He began throwing people off of him as they tried to hold him on the ground, scouring backward across the ground like a whipped animal. His eyes were wide open, and his face revealed sheer terror. Those who related the story said he was as afraid as a man being driven into the flames.

Eventually, he calmed down enough to tell with quivering lips what had occurred. As he told the story, between hard breaths, he would turn his head and shriek as if fearful of something attacking him from behind. He finally said that as he tried to light the final match and it fizzled out, an angel from God was standing directly in his face and said something so loudly to him that he thought the entire world must have heard it. Paralyzed momentarily in fear, he stared into the eyes of this messenger, which proclaimed, "I am a messenger of the Most High God sent to warn you so that you will warn others that this is God's real holy ground, and you will die if you do not flee."

As the pastor related this powerful story to me over the cell phone, I stood in the airport. I began crying, and as I was listening, I could hear the pastor say, "Brother, can you hear something? Do you hear the man yelling behind me now while we are talking?" I could faintly make out the voice of someone yelling in the far distance over the phone, but I was unable to make out his words. On the other end of the line, the pastor was holding his cell phone out in the air to pick up the voice of the man. He was yelling in his native language, and I was unable to interpret. The pastor told me it was the actual man who had that morning attempted to burn the church down. He was going from rooftop to rooftop and screaming his story to everyone, causing large numbers of salvations in the village yards and under trees! It reminded me of the verse in the Bible, "Let the angel of the Lord chase them."

This amazing story indicates that God is concerned for His people and will initiate a judgment against those who would harm His followers or destroy His church!

—PERRY STONE, *Angels on Assignment*

ANGELS EXECUTE JUDGMENT

By Ron Phillips

NGELIC ACTIVITY ERUPTS at the mighty epochs of God's kingdom. Angels sang and shouted as God called the creation out of nothing (Job 38:1–7). Angels conveyed the glory of God with a backslidden Judah to Babylonian captivity. Angels covered God's ancient people during their captivity. Angels welcomed the Messiah above Bethlehem fields with a sound and light show not seen since Creation (Luke 2:8–20). Sadly, the same angels who raised the curtain on our planet and have guarded its destiny will also release the judgments that are yet to come.

GOD'S WRATH FULLY RELEASED

The last book in the Bible records two phenomena intensifying at the same time. Worship intensifies in a powerful crescendo that shakes all of creation. Conversely, wars and catastrophes intensify. God will judge every failed human system and then every human being outside of Christ. Angelic activity in judging nations and in times of war is evident in Scripture and history. In 1 Chronicles 21, one angel stretched his sword over Jerusalem, and seventy thousand men of Israel died in a plague. Angels announced the judgment of Sodom and Gomorrah in Genesis 19. In 2 Kings 19, Hezekiah prayed, and one warring angel killed one hundred eighty-five thousand Assyrians, thwarting their occupation of Israel. In Acts 12, an angel struck down King Herod because of his pride. Only in the next life will we understand how many dictators, presidents, kings, sheikhs, and prime ministers have had their careers affected by angels. Furthermore, we will know then how many battles were won or lost at the hand of the angel allies. Perhaps then we will understand the angelic involvement that has swayed the nations.

All of these judgments pale in comparison to the end-time scenario of Revelation. Angels are the enforcers of God's wrath on the cursed earth. When we turn the pages of Revelation, there is an explosion of angelic activity like never before witnessed on Earth. In the opening three chapters, angels are assigned to the church and are active in communicating God's will. In Revelation chapters 4 and 5 angels join all of creation in the most majestic worship service ever assembled.

After that phenomenal worship, angels begin to blow trumpets that summon horrific judgments on the planet. As we continue to read in Revelation 6, we see the horror of wars, famines, plagues, and natural disasters claim one-third of the human population of earth. Interestingly, at the sixth trumpet, angels of judgment bound in the river Euphrates are released to kill that one-third of humanity mentioned earlier. Yes, from Iraq, ancient Babylon will issue horrific bloodshed on Earth.

As we continue to turn the pages of Revelation we see an extreme intensification occur. Chapters 15 through 16 of Revelation record the pouring out of seven bowls of wrath on the earth. Images such as the river of blood brought on by angelic actions are terrifying. Angels will bring down false religions, and it is angels who judge the great religious harlot in Revelation 17:1–2: "One of the seven angels who had the seven bowls came and talked with me, saying to me, 'Come, I will show you the judgment of the great prostitute who sits on many waters, with whom the kings of the earth committed adultery, and the inhabitants of the earth were made drunk with the wine of her sexual immorality.'"

Angels announce the collapse of Wall Street and all other world markets. The fear that gripped our nation in these current seasons of recession and depression is nothing in comparison to that final hour.

> After this I saw another angel coming down from heaven,
> having great authority, and the earth was illuminated
> with his glory. He cried out mightily with a loud voice,
> saying: "'Fallen! Fallen is Babylon the Great!'" She has
> become a dwelling place of demons, a haunt for every
> unclean spirit, and a haunt for every unclean and hateful
> bird. For all the nations have drunk of the wine of the
> wrath of her sexual immorality, the kings of the earth
> have committed adultery with her, and the merchants
> of the earth have become rich through the abundance
> of her luxury." Then I heard another voice from heaven
> saying: "'Come out of her, my people,' lest you partake
> in her sins, and lest you receive her plagues."
>
> —REVELATION 18:1–4

All of the greed, thievery, and luxury will be brought down by the angels of God.

On the final pages of Revelation, angels accompany our Lord Jesus at His Second Coming. The mighty hosts of heaven who are His palace guards come to "mop up" the remaining foes on Earth. Paul describes that scene vividly: "And to give you who are troubled rest with us when the Lord Jesus is revealed from heaven with His mighty angels, in flaming fire taking vengeance on those who do not know God and do not obey the gospel of our Lord Jesus Christ" (2 Thess. 1:7–8). The Lord will come with mighty angels to finish off the enemy. Angels will implement the death of the wicked.

God will avenge His people at the revelation of Jesus Christ. Our Lord will be revealed with His "mighty angels." The word *mighty* translates *dunamis*, which means "explosive power." These angels will come in *phlox pur*, or "flaming fire," to purify the universe and punish the wicked! Second Thessalonians 1:9 says this punishment will be "eternal destruction, isolated from the presence of the Lord."

Then Satan will be captured and contained by one mighty angel.

And I saw an angel coming down out of heaven, having the key to the bottomless pit and a great chain in his hand. He seized the dragon, that ancient serpent, who is the Devil and Satan, and bound him for a thousand years. He cast him into the bottomless pit, and shut him up, and set a seal on him, that he should deceive the nations no more, until the thousand years were ended. After that he must be set free for a little while.

…The devil, who deceived them, was cast into the lake of fire and brimstone where the beast and the false prophet were. They will be tormented day and night forever and ever.

—Revelation 20:1–3, 10

All of the unsaved will be cast into hell by angels! Let the idea that angels are small effervescent creatures fluttering around leave you forever. Angels are mighty warriors and, in the last days, will execute God's wrath without mercy!

Finally, angels will announce the rapture of the church. Our glorious translation will remove the final restraint, and God will unleash the final judgment: "For the Lord Himself will descend from heaven with a shout, with the voice of the archangel, and with the trumpet call of God. And the dead in Christ will rise first" (1 Thess. 4:16).

Examples of Angels Sending Judgment

The New Testament records an unusual event involving an angel who brought judgment against a national leader. Luke records a political event where as Herod sat upon his throne, the people screamed that he was not a man but a god (Acts 12:20–22). The historian Josephus wrote about the event also with these words:

On the second day of which shows he put on a garment made wholly of silver, and of a contexture truly wonderful, and came into the theater early in the morning; at which time the silver of his garment being illuminated by the fresh reflection of the sun's rays upon it, shone out after a surprising manner, and was so resplendent as to spread a horror over those that looked intently upon him; and presently his flatterers cried out...that he was a god...the king did neither rebuke them...A severe pain also arose in his belly, and began in a most violent manner.

—ANTIQUITIES OF THE JEWS,
BOOK 19, CHAPTER 8, SECTION 2

Luke recorded that when the people glorified Herod as a god, an "angel of the Lord struck him, because he did not give glory to God. And he was eaten by worms" (Acts 12:23). Josephus reported that the pains became violent, and in five days the king was dead at age fifty-four. We don't often picture angels as being initiators of God's judgment, but in the Book of Revelation, John reports seeing angels pouring out the judgments during the Great Tribulation (Rev. 8:2; 15:1). God's will in heaven is performed on Earth and is often linked to the assignments given to angels. While angels may bring judgment upon the ungodly and wicked, they will also bring warnings to the righteous.

—PERRY STONE, *Angels on Assignment*

ANGELS SING A SONG OF END-TIMES DISASTERS

Further proof of angelic activity in the last days is a story a missionary to China tells about angels warning of end-times disaster through rural Chinese churchgoers who were singing in the Spirit during a 1995 worship service. The account reads as follows:

The whole province of Shandong, in eastern China (population: 57 million), is in the midst of a sweeping revival. For fear of arrest, believers meet secretly in house churches, often by candlelight. At a 1995 meeting in Shandong, everyone was singing "in the Spirit" together (1 Corinthians 14:15), not in their own language, but "as the Spirit gave them utterance," all in harmony but all singing different words.

Someone audiotaped the meeting. Later, when they played back the cassette, they were shocked! What they heard was not what had happened there at all—but the sound of angels singing in Mandarin—a song they had never heard before, and with a musical accompaniment that had not been there!!! When my friend first heard the tape, before anyone told him what it was, he exclaimed, "Those are angels!!" Actually, there was no other explanation. A Chinese Christian coworker translated the tape. Below are the actual words sung by the angels! Note that the words express ideas with which these rural Chinese peasants were not familiar.

The End Is Near: Rescue Souls

The famine is becoming more and more critical. There are more and more earthquakes. The situation is becoming more and more sinister. People are fighting against each other, nation against nation. Disasters are more and more severe.

The whole environment is deteriorating. Disasters are more and more severe. People's hearts are wicked, and they do not worship the true God. Disasters are more and more severe.

Floods and droughts are more and more frequent. There is more and more homosexuality and incurable diseases. Disasters are more and more severe.

The climates are becoming more and more abnormal. The earth is more and more restless.

The skies have been broken. The atmosphere is distorted. Disasters are more and more severe.

Chorus

The end is near. The revelation of love has been manifested. Rise up, rise up, rescue souls. The end is near. Rise up, rise up, rescue souls.[1]

GOD'S WRATH ON SATAN RELEASED AT THE CROSS

While I have shown through Scripture and real-life events that wars and catastrophes increase toward the close of time, let me make it clear that all demonic spirits are already defeated. At the cross and empty tomb, Christ won a transdimensional, cosmic victory over all the forces of darkness. The Bible affirms this truth. At Jesus's ascension, He laid claim to full authority in heaven and earth: "Then Jesus came and spoke to them, saying, 'All authority has been given to Me in heaven and on earth'" (Matt. 28:18).

In a cosmic display of power, Jesus stripped the forces of darkness of their rights and authority: "...He blotted out the handwriting of ordinances that was against us and contrary to us, and He took it out of the way, nailing it to the cross. And having disarmed authorities and powers, He made a show of them openly, triumphing over them by the cross" (Col. 2:14–15).

He destroyed the devil's threat of death and his right to hold captive those who come to Christ: "So then, as the children share in flesh and blood, He likewise took part in these, so that through death He might destroy him who has the power of death, that is, the devil, and deliver those who through fear of death were throughout their lives subject to bondage" (Heb. 2:14–15).

All of the forces of darkness are subject to Jesus. As we have seen, Jesus has defeated them all in the eternal realms; we are here to enforce the victory already won. "...who has gone into heaven and is at the right hand of God, with angels and authorities and powers being made subject to Him" (1 Pet. 3:22).

The enemy is subject to Jesus but not subject to those who are not Christ's followers.

Though the war is won, we must enforce the victory of Christ. One of the reasons the enemy is here is to train followers for the future world. More significantly, the enemy is here for you to defeat him and display God's wisdom in saving you.

History has an example that might help you understand this concept. The War of 1812 was over, and peace agreements had been reached when the Battle of New Orleans was fought. Andrew Jackson led the army to a great victory in New Orleans; however, one of the greatest battles of that century served no purpose beyond that of making Andrew Jackson president.

Likewise, our victory was won by Jesus Christ at the cross and the empty tomb. Yet, like the War of 1812 and the Battle of New Orleans, we are still in a battle, even though the war has been won. However, in this battle, we have the privilege to fight alongside our angel allies who enforce the victory already won!

The war is won, but we are in the final countdown to its finish. The Scriptures are very clear on the angelic actions at the end of the age, especially in the Book of Revelation where angelic activity is recorded on almost every page. We can be confident in our God who has already announced the victory and set His war plan in writing in Scripture.

PART IV

How Angels Are Activated

Chapter 23

THROUGH GOD'S COMMAND

By Ron Phillips

NGELS ARE ASSIGNED the responsibility to serve believers. When a believer operates as an heir to the kingdom of God, then angels are sent to serve. Our failure to activate angelic assistance has limited our growth and success in our mission enterprise. There is a powerful word on angels found in Hebrews 1:14. It says, "Are they not all ministering spirits sent out to minister to those who will inherit salvation?" The phrase "sent forth" is the Greek word *apostello,* which is the same word translated as "apostle." Angels are sent forth with those who are willing to "go forth." The phrase "sent forth" means to be sent out with a commission. Angels protect and endorse the message God is speaking today by using their authority. The phrase also speaks of the apostolic, prophetic, and evangelistic work done as they help spread the good news.

ANGELS GIVE INSTRUCTIONS

I had just turned twenty-one years old and was experiencing one of the most exciting times in my young life. I was a newly married student at Samford University and had just begun a new ministry at a church in Wilsonville, Alabama. As I drove to Birmingham for a long day of classes, I noticed a young man hitchhiking. Normally, I never stop for hitchhikers; however, on this day I stopped for the young man.

As I watched him get in my car, he said, "Now worship Jesus Christ."

Then he said, "I must tell you something. You will have an

awakening, and you will baptize dozens of people. Do not be dismayed if the old church does not receive all that God releases. You are appointed here for the purpose of touching the people no one wants."

He then asked me to let him out of the car. As he got out of the car, I said, "God bless you."

He looked at me, smiled, and said, "He already has, and He has blessed you!"

Two weeks later we baptized thirty-six new converts; most of them lived in a poor community of small shotgun houses. The church did not receive them, but God put a love in my heart, from that moment until now, for the needy and outcast. I believe I encountered an angel.

Angels go before us on life's journey toward our promised destiny. In Exodus 33:2, God said, "I will send an angel before you, and I will drive out the Canaanite, the Amorite, the Hittite, the Perizzite, the Hivite, and the Jebusite." It is comforting to know that the Lord is directing our way and that His angels take each step before us. There are angelic scouts exploring and preparing the way ahead.

Angel Spies

I am a real seeker of answers from God. My attitude is always, "God, just tell me what to do, and I will do it!" So when I have a problem or am in a difficult situation, I just tell Him, "Give me the path, the strategy; tell me how to do it step by step, and I will take care of it."

That has been my continual cry for years, and God always answers me. As I started getting into more complicated situations, I needed more complicated answers.

I remember one night when God was speaking to me, He said, "I want you to call forth 'the spies.'" I didn't understand that at all. Spies? What is that? So I asked Him to explain what He meant.

I went to an online Bible study program and typed in "spies." It brought up Numbers 21, the account of when the Israelites as a nation actually entered the Promised Land to occupy it. They did so via the route of Atharim (v. 1). This is the route the twelve spies of Israel had previously taken when they went into the land to spy it out and see if it was good.

Years later when Israel finally entered the Promised Land, they found this same path the spies had taken. It was the route that led them in to possess the land. The Israelites knew how to return into the Promised Land because the spies had already been there.

As I read that scripture, the Lord told me "the spies" He told me to call forth are an actual angelic force. When you call for them, you release them to go before you, to find the route, which is the specific way you need to go to get to your promised land. They go ahead of you and come back to release the directions to you. They may say, "Go right here," "Go left here," "Go up here," or "Go down there." That is their job. They are the spies who give you the directions, the way to get into your promised land.

At different times since this discovery and understanding, the Lord has told me to "Call forth the spies!" I call them and release these angelic spies. In a matter of weeks I begin to get revelation and answers to a problem. Then I am able to take hold of the answer, which takes me in and gives me entry into a new area of my promised land.

A specific example of this is once when I needed a really big miracle, a big breakthrough. I needed specific directions on how to get into an area of my promised land. So I prayed, and I released the spies.

Then one night I was in my kitchen at home, not doing anything spiritual, mind you; I was just making a peanut butter and banana sandwich. I wasn't even praying or thinking much about my situation or even thinking about God. But suddenly the spies appeared in my kitchen. I could actually see them.

These angel spies were right there in front of me. They all wore safari outfits, as if they had been on a safari. They wore hats on their heads and carried guns, binoculars, maps, and everything else you would need if you were going on a journey to chart a way. They talked amongst themselves as I just sat there watching them in total amazement. I could see them with my eyes open, and even though they were very obvious to me and very easy to see, they were transparent, not solid. I could see them and see through them at the same time. They stood there for a moment, talking and doing things amongst themselves, and then, just like that, they disappeared.

The next day I began to get a major revelation for a huge breakthrough I had been waiting on for a long time. In fact, since that moment in my kitchen, I have seen countless miracles occur through the strategies released when the angel spies show up.

—KATIE SOUZA, AUTHOR, SPEAKER, AND
FOUNDER OF EXPECTED END MINISTRIES

ANGELS WARN BELIEVERS

Remember, the angel warned Joseph of Herod's evil intention: "Now when they departed, the angel of the Lord appeared to Joseph in a dream, saying, 'Arise, take the young Child and His mother, and escape to Egypt, and stay there until I bring you word. For Herod will seek the young Child to kill Him'" (Matt. 2:13). Throughout history angels have waved red flags in front of believers, and we can count on that same protective intervention in our lives today.

Bart was on his way to Branson, Missouri, for the annual Yamaha motorcycle convention when he had an unbelievable encounter he will never forget. He was traveling on his motorcycle behind a semi-truck, going seventy to seventy-five miles an hour when he heard a clear voice inside of him say, "Switch lanes to the left."

As soon as he had completed the lane change, the semitrailer in front of him blew a rear tire and scattered large pieces of tread in the right lane, where he had been just moments before. Bart honestly believes that if it were not for that divine intervention telling him to switch lanes, he would not be alive today. He probably would have crashed into the back of the semi or flipped the bike after hitting the separated tread.

That day Bart is sure that he heard his angel tell him, clear as a bell, to switch lanes because there was trouble ahead.[1]

ANGELS ARE WATCHING

When we bind the enemy and loose our allies, the angels do the work for us. Many times the church, collectively and as individuals, does not stand on its position in Christ. As a result, we fail to engage the legions of angels standing ready to assist. Matthew 16:19 puts it like this: "I will give you the keys of the kingdom of heaven, and whatever you bind on earth shall be bound in heaven, and whatever you loose on earth shall be loosed in heaven." As believers operate, they must understand that angelic assistance is a key to kingdom power in the earth. These wonderful beings are the agents of God who operate in opening doors and binding the curses.

The mighty hosts of heaven are called watchers in Scripture. I am convinced that angels can reveal international crises and international needs. As watchers, they are looking out for all believers! Angels are God's scouts on the earth doing reconnaissance. In Zechariah chapter 1, we find the angels walking to and fro, or to put it in more contemporary language, walking back and forth throughout the earth keeping watch over creation. This night they had a good report: "We have gone to and fro on the earth, and all the earth is resting and peaceful" (Zech. 1:11).

The prophet Daniel also calls angels watchers. They are doing surveillance over all creation. Above our earth are man-made satellites recording global activities; in a greater way, angels are also watching over us. "I saw in the visions of my head upon my bed, and there was a holy watcher coming down from heaven" (Dan. 4:13).

I was chatting with my recently widowed mother-in-law, a faithful Christian, about living alone. She has opted to stay in the large house where she and my father-in-law, Billy, had lived so long. She quickly told me she was not afraid. With a shy smile, she said, "I know that angels are watching over me."

When Billy was in his last living moments, there in their home with all the family gathered around, he opened his blue eyes and looked heavenward as a glory filled the room. Billy then closed his eyes and went to heaven. Though not visible, an angel had come to transport him home to glory, and I firmly believe angels have stayed with my mother-in-law, Polly, ever since.

Angels are always on guard, covering the earth. They report on all that they observe on the earth. If we are on the right channel, we too can have wisdom on what God is doing in the earth.

Chapter 14

THROUGH SCRIPTURE

By Ron Phillips

OR MORE THAN thirty years I have served as pastor of Abba's House. During that time I have prepared and delivered over five thousand messages, which totals over sixty-five thousand written pages. I have written more than fifteen books and have taught daily radio for over ten of those years, which equal more than three thousand messages. During all this time, I can honestly say that most people who heard these scriptural messages didn't respond. However, it is encouraging to know that not a single angel disobeyed the Word of God that came forth from my mouth.

Angels are activated by the Word of God and move accordingly. They don't do as we humans sometimes do—respond to God's commands reluctantly or depending on how we feel about what He is asking. When God speaks, they act. Angels reverence, respect, and respond to the Word of God. They have a special interest in presenting, protecting, proclaiming, and performing the Word of God. Angels will not violate the written Word of God; they are committed to its dictates. In most cases when angelic involvement occurs, a message from heaven is being delivered. Angels know that the messages they deliver change the destiny of nations and are of life-and-death importance.

ANGELS AND THE ORIGIN OF SCRIPTURE

Scripture speaks of their heavenly origin. Scripture is the God-breathed writings of men giving witness to the mighty acts of God:

"All Scripture is inspired by God and is profitable for teaching, for reproof, for correction, and for instruction in righteousness" (2 Tim. 3:16).

In this verse Paul declares the writings of the Bible to be God breathed. The Holy Spirit actively superintended the writing of Scripture. Simon Peter affirmed that Scripture came from God to humanity: "And we have a more reliable word of prophecy, which you would do well to follow, as to a light that shines in a dark place, until the day dawns and the morning star arises in your hearts. But know this first of all, that no prophecy of the Scripture is a matter of one's own interpretation. For no prophecy at any time was produced by the will of man, but holy men moved by the Holy Spirit spoke from God" (2 Pet. 1:19–21).

Beyond the connection between God and man, we find an ally in the formation of Scripture, the holy angels. The angels were deeply involved in the giving of the Word. When Moses ascended Mount Sinai, he was met by an innumerable company of angels, who participated in the revelation of the Law: "And he said: 'The LORD came from Sinai, and dawned on them from Seir; He shone forth from Mount Paran, and He came with ten thousands of saints; from His right hand came a fiery law for them'" (Deut. 33:2, NKJV). The word *saints* is "holy ones," and scholars agree that it is a reference to angels.[1]

Psalm 68:17 affirms the angelic covering at Mount Sinai when Moses conferred with God about the Law that would become the bedrock of human civilization: "The chariots of God are twice ten thousand, even thousands of thousands; the Lord is among them, as in Sinai, in the holy place."

When you turn to the pages of the New Testament, you find a clear affirmation of angelic assistance with the Scriptures, especially the Law. The deacon Stephen, in his sermon that resulted in his martyrdom, declared the same truth: "...who have received the law by the direction of angels and have not kept it" (Acts 7:53, NKJV).

The Law came "by the direction of the angels." The apostle Paul, in writing to the Galatian church, said the Law was "appointed" by angels: "What purpose then does the law serve? It was added because of transgressions, till the Seed should come to whom the promise was made; and it was appointed through angels by the hand of a mediator" (Gal. 3:19, NKJV).

Furthermore, the writer of Hebrews declares the absolute integrity of the "word spoken through angels": "For if the word spoken through angels proved steadfast, and every transgression and disobedience received a just reward…" (Heb. 2:2, NKJV).

Angels participated in the giving of the Law, and they also carried out the sentences of the Law.

ANGELS ENFORCE THE WORD

Look again Hebrews 2:2 (NKJV): "For if the word spoken through angels proved steadfast, and every transgression and disobedience received a just reward…" The word *transgression* means to trespass, to go beyond the ordinary boundary; indeed, "to break the rules." *Disobedience* means simply to act against what has been commanded. Angels punish lawbreakers! This is why you must never assign angelic protection in your life if you are violating the Law and disobeying authority. It is abundantly clear that angels respect, respond, and release the Word of God.

As we have observed, the angels were present at the giving of the Law (Ps. 68:17), the Law came by angelic direction (Acts 7:53), the Law was "appointed through angels" (Gal. 3:19), and the Word was "spoken" in some cases by the angels (Heb. 2:2). We conclude from these scriptures that obedience to the Word of God is vital to release angelic activity. Also, could it be possible that angels are grieved by humans who transgress God's laws? Both angels and demons are arranged in military hierarchy; therefore, rebellion would be considered grievous. Could it be that angelic help is stifled by rebellious activity?

Angels Give Heed to God's Word

The psalmist wrote, "Bless the LORD, you His angels, who excel in strength, who do His word, heeding the voice of His word" (Ps. 103:20, NKJV). Angels are assigned to perform the word or instructions God gives them.

They are also interested in hearing the Word of God preached by mortal men. Peter wrote: "To them it was revealed that, not to themselves, but to us they were ministering the things which now have been reported to you through those who have preached the gospel to you by the Holy Spirit sent from heaven—things which angels desire to look into"(1 Pet. 1:12, NKJV).

—PERRY STONE, *Angels on Assignment*

ANGELS AND THE CONFESSED WORD

Moving from the negative to the positive, we see that angels are activated and released when we confess, by faith, the Word of God: "Bless the LORD, you His angels, who excel in strength, who do His word, heeding the voice of His word. Bless the LORD, all you His hosts, you ministers of His, who do His pleasure" (Ps. 103:20–21, NKJV). This scripture gives us clear direction on how angels are moved by God's Word. Notice that the Word is powerfully embraced by the hosts of heaven in an atmosphere of worship. When a believer worships, angels gather.

Secondly, angels "do His word." This is their vocation and purpose. Angels will cause the Word of God to come to pass in the lives of believers.

Third, notice that when the Word is voiced, angels are activated. When a faithful Christian says aloud the Word God has released in him or her, that Word is carried forth on the wings of angels to be answered. Angels do God's Word and respond to the Word spoken aloud! Angels cannot read your mind. When you confess the Word of God by faith out of your mouth, angels move instantly. It is their joy to speedily bring your confession to pass! As we obey, heed, and confess the Word of God, we bring our angelic allies into full partnership. They will bring to pass what God has promised.

At a staff meeting in our church some years ago, there was a report of a financial need. I prayed and dispatched harvest angels to go get what God's Word had promised us. Before the meeting ended, a local businessman brought in a five-figure check that met the need. God's angels moved when the promise of God's Word was embraced and spoken.

Angels Deliver New Body Parts

In a service once when I saw an angel for the very first time with my physical eyes, I thought at first I was looking at a cloud, like a glory cloud. I rubbed my eyes, trying to figure it out. I thought, "What is that? Am I having a weird vision, or is this my imagination?" I couldn't really tell.

These angels were going over the congregation, over the people in the church, and I was seeing them, but they looked kind of weird to me. And "weird" is really an understatement, but it is the only way I can describe them. These angels didn't have wings; they had an arm span. They were gliding, like flying, over the congregation, and each of them had a big hump on his back. I couldn't figure it out; I couldn't make out what that hump was. It was like I was seeing deformed angels, but I'd never seen or heard of that.

Then, suddenly I said, "In the name of Jesus, somebody over here needs a heart. In the name of Jesus I send the word of healing. I send a new heart in Jesus's name." And instantly I saw this angel reach backward into the hump, and at that moment the person I was praying for moved abruptly as if he had been hit by something. In that moment he received a brand-new heart.

The humps on the backs of the angels were like backpacks. There were body parts in there! God showed me He had body parts for the people in the service. "This is awesome!" I thought.

So I just kept going, and I just kept praying. I saw a man and said, "New lungs," and the angel reached behind into the hump and the man got new lungs! We all saw him react like he'd been hit! He took a really deep breath—*haaa*—and said, "I can breathe!"

That's how the night went. It was *way* cool!

People who have had experiences going to heaven sometimes report that there are warehouses full of body parts. My position is that I do not want any body part left in the heavenly warehouse! As for anyone who comes to my service, I want them to get their new body part; that's for sure. And God just does it.

He has given knees, elbows, lungs, shoulders, hearts, prostates, intestines, even a back. One person received the part of their colon that had been taken out. It is just awesome.

I don't know how God does it. I just know that He does.

That first time I saw the angels gliding over the congregation, reaching into the humps on their backs and delivering new body parts, also was my first experience personally ministering with and seeing these angels. But now they go with me wherever I go; and when I am praying, anointing, and imparting, there is an infusion of the anointing power of healing, and God sends the healing angels.

—Joan Hunter, author and healing evangelist
with Joan Hunter Ministries

Chapter 15

THROUGH PRAYER

By Ron Phillips

NGELIC ACTIVITY SWIRLS around and mingles with things of the Spirit. We have already observed how angels are connected to the glory of worship and to the needs of believers. Angels are especially attuned to the spiritual discipline of prayer. Angels are activated by a sincere heart seeking God in prayer. It appears in Scripture that angelic worship includes watching over the prayers of believers. On two occasions angels are viewed as attending the prayers of believers.

First, in the dramatic worship scene found in Revelation 5, the Lamb takes the scroll from the strong angel. This scroll recounts all of the trials of humanity across the ages. Only our Lord Jesus, by His sacrifice, can restore what has been lost. In this powerful vision, the Lamb bears the visible signs of having been slain. (See Revelation 5:6–7.)

When the Lion/Lamb seizes the scroll, triumphant worship breaks out among those redeemed and among the heavenly hosts. As the praise begins, there is a mysterious mention of angels and our prayers: "When He had taken the scroll, the four living creatures and the twenty-four elders fell down before the Lamb, each one having a harp, and golden bowls full of incense, which are the prayers of saints" (Rev. 5:8).

It appears the prayers of all believers across all time are being watched over by angels. Prayers are viewed as "golden bowls" of "incense." This image takes us back to temple worship where the incense burned before the cloud of glory, God's presence. Angels keep our prayers as a sweet smell before the throne of God. Prayers are cherished in heaven and are in the care of the worshipping hosts. In the Scripture reference above, the angel hosts play their harps (*kithara* in the Greek, from which we get the English word *guitar*). As they play and lead worship, the prayers ascend as incense before the throne of God: "The smoke of the incense, with the prayers of the saints, ascended before God from the angel's hand. Then the angel took the censer, filled it with fire from the altar, and threw it onto the earth. And there were noises, thundering, lightning, and an earthquake" (Rev. 8:4–5).

As this scene unfolds, the prayers of believers loose the seven trumpets of judgment on the earth. Notice our prayers "ascended before God from the angel's hand." Then our prayers are hurled back to the earth as fire! This powerful image of prayer is confirmed in Psalm 141:1–2: "LORD, I cry unto You; make haste to me; give ear to my voice, when I cry unto You. Let my prayer be set forth before You as incense, and the lifting up of my hands as the evening sacrifice." Notice the image of incense and prayer. Angels of worship attend to the sincere cries of God's people.

Angels Are Moved by Our Prayers

The Scriptures record an amazing incident in the life of the Hebrew prophet Daniel: "Then he said to me, 'Do not fear, Daniel, for from the first day that you set your heart to understand, and to humble yourself before your God, your words were heard; and I have come because of your words. But the prince of the kingdom of Persia withstood me twenty-one days; and behold, Michael, one of the chief princes, came to help me, for I had been left alone there with the kings of Persia'" (Dan. 10:12–13, NKJV).

Daniel had been forced out of his homeland in Israel to serve the king of Babylon during Israel's seventy years of captivity to King Nebuchadnezzar and other kings of the Babylonian empire. Under Daniel's watch, there were several prophetic dreams and visions that were revealed to both the king and Daniel. On one occasion, Daniel was unable to receive the understanding to a strange and disturbing prophetic vision. This resulted in a long, twenty-one-day fast and a season of prayer to beseech God for a clear understanding of the unknown.

For three full weeks, Daniel fasted and prayed and was unable to break through the heavens, which were like brass. He was unaware that two opposing angels were engaged in a cosmic conflict in the atmospheric heavens just above the metropolis of Babylon. Eventually, God's messenger (many believe it was Gabriel) called for reinforcements and was assisted directly by the archangel Michael, who restrained a spirit called the *prince of the kingdom of Persia*. This demonic entity was what Paul later identified as a principality (Eph. 6:12), which is a chief ruling spirit that influences governments over nations, cities, or provinces.

The angel revealed that he had come to Daniel because of his "words." These words were the prayers the prophet had sent up to the heavenly temple, asking God to bring the understanding. Gabriel is the chief angel that reveals specific revelation from the throne of God and had previously appeared twice to Daniel, giving the Hebrew prophet insight into prophetic events that would unfold in the future. (See Daniel 8:16; 9:21.) The Bible is clear that at times God sends answers to prayers through angels.

In the time of the second temple, there was a priest named Zacharias. His wife, Elizabeth, a cousin to Mary the mother of Christ, was an older woman and had never conceived. One morning while Zacharias was burning incense on the golden altar at the temple in Jerusalem, the angel Gabriel appeared on the right side of the altar with a message that Zacharias's wife, Elizabeth, would conceive and birth a son named *John*, who would come in the "spirit and power of Elijah" (Luke 1:4–17). Zacharias was frightened, perhaps because he was to be alone in the holy place when offering incense, and this *stranger* had entered, which could cause God's judgment to suddenly strike them both. Second, in Jewish tradition, the right side of the altar was reserved for God Himself. Perhaps Zacharias was fearful of dying if this was the Lord who was appearing! The angel announced, "Do not be afraid, Zacharias, for your prayer is heard" (Luke 1:13).

Here was a priest from the temple burning incense on the golden altar, which according to Scripture represents the prayers of the saints going up to God in His heavenly temple. The psalmist knew this when he wrote, "Let my prayer be set before You as incense, the lifting up of my hands as the evening sacrifice" (Ps. 141:2). How amazing that while Zacharias is presenting the prayer of others before God, the Lord answers his own prayer at the golden altar.

—PERRY STONE, *Angels on Assignment*

NO PRAYER GOES UNNOTICED

Angels collect all of our prayers, and they are offered as a sacrifice to God. Until the answer is ready, they burn before the throne of God as a sweet sacrifice. Angels tend our prayers and are agents used to answer our prayers. In due season the Holy Spirit and the angels of fire move to answer the righteous prayers of believers. A clear example of how this works is recorded in Luke 1:8–12.

Zacharias was serving as the high priest and ministering by burning incense as all the people were in the outer court of the temple praying at the hour of incense. The people knew that prayer mixed with sacrifice and worship was powerful and effective. In that moment the invisible works of God became visible. Astonishingly, the angel of the Lord stood at the right side of the altar of incense. What was this angel doing? He was gathering the prayers of believers as he always did, but on that day he manifested himself to Zacharias. Why did the angel show himself? Because Zacharias and Elizabeth had been praying earnestly all their lives for a child. At the hour of incense, the hour of prayer, the angel who watches over prayer showed up. This scene ends with a fearful Zacharias doubting the word from Gabriel and being struck mute so he could not confess unbelief and contradict the word of faith claimed by his wife, Elizabeth. Angels respond to "the voice of His word" (Ps. 103:20); therefore, Gabriel would not allow a single word of unbelief to be voiced during Elizabeth's pregnancy.

Consider the following story of a woman's answered prayer:

> My husband and oldest son work at the same place in Colusa, California. We live in Colusa, and our son lives thirty miles away. They work early hours. One morning after my husband left for work I could not sleep. I looked at the clock and it was 4:45 a.m. Our son was on my mind and heavy on my heart. I just thought I was being overprotective and tried to close my eyes to go back to sleep.
>
> The weight got so heavy I could not lie down anymore. I called my husband at work and asked him if our son had gotten to work yet. He said no. By this time it was 5:20 a.m. and he was to start at 5:30. I started praying and asking God to please put His angels around my son and get him safely to work.
>
> I was still praying for God's angels when, about twenty minutes later, I heard a car outside. As I opened the front door, my son was walking up to the door. His car was still running, driver's door open, and his head in his hands. He was crying, and he said, "Mom, I almost died."
>
> He had fallen asleep at the wheel as he was crossing a two-mile bridge. As the road curved, his car went

straight into the other lane and hit the cement wall. The car then lifted about one inch from the top of the wall. He woke up and struggled to back the car off the wall, scraping it for at least ten feet.

I hugged my son, and I told him what happened to me earlier and that I had prayed for God's angels to protect him. We both cried and thanked God for giving him a guardian angel.[1]

Waiting for Someone to Pray

One night my wife and I were with some friends, about a dozen of us, worshipping and praying. We had come together because of one couple who were experiencing tremendous spiritual warfare. They were seeing some really demonic stuff. So during this time we were all in prayer together for them.

All of sudden, in a single moment, *bam!* I and one other guy were taken up in the Spirit! It was unique because we experienced it together. This other guy and I were in the Spirit together, seeing the same things at the same time. Everyone else in the room could hear our voices describing what was going on because our bodies were still there in the room. But our spirits had been taken to another realm, and we were with God the Father.

In that realm we were able to take a survey of what was happening on the dark side around the family we had gathered to pray for. We were able to see exactly what was going on, and we called out, "God! Send Your angels!" Then *whoomp*—like a flash of lightning, as far as our eyes could see, angelic hosts started showing up. They were warring angels. I mean, they were buff angels with massive swords, and their armor was polished so brightly that it was almost white.

One angel stepped forward and said, "We have been waiting for someone to pray." My only response was, "*Whoa!*"

This angel resumed his position, and the host of angels went off, and all of a sudden we could see a war taking place. We were able to watch this war between the angelic hosts of God and the dark spirits. It was a literal war, taking place in the heavenlies. We watched it go on for several minutes over this family's house and their neighborhood. We couldn't believe it; it was so real. It was *real*.

As I thought about it afterward, it brought to mind what Paul wrote in 1 Thessalonians 5:17, "Pray without ceasing." We don't know what our prayers actually are activating!

That evening I got to see a reality of what happens when we pray. I saw that, as we prayed and asked the Father to release His angels on behalf of this family—on behalf of what was going on, against the way of darkness—we were able to actually see the hosts of heaven come in and just explode and erupt over that family and their home and their entire household.

—STEVEN SPRINGER, SENIOR LEADER WITH HIS WIFE, RENE, OF GLOBAL PRESENCE MINISTRIES IN MADISON, WISCONSIN

WHAT DOES ALL THIS SAY TO US?

1. Angels abide in the secret place of prayer.

2. Angels are stirred and motivated by both individual and corporate prayer.

3. Prayer is best offered in a context of intense worship.

4. Angels watch over prayers yet to be answered.

5. Prayers are a pleasant and sweet aroma to God our Father.

6. Prayers rise to God from the hands of our angel allies.

7. Angels respond negatively to wrong words; negative confessions, curses, and unbelief hinder the miracle-working Word.

8. Prayers offered in passionate faith and trust in God will be answered by God and delivered by angels.

Your prayers matter to our Father and activate angelic assistance. Remember, no prayer goes unnoticed or unanswered. I realize to some of you that doesn't make sense, when you have prayed for healing and the healing hasn't come, or when you have suffered greatly and there seemed to be no relief. However, the passages we discussed in this chapter show us that our prayers have been entrusted to angels until their appointed time. As allies with the angels, we must be reassured by the power of prayer and spend time regularly with God.

THROUGH KINGDOM MINISTRY

By Ron Phillips

NGELIC ACTIVITY IS on the increase in these last days. The reason for supernatural operations is twofold. First, as we move toward the end, human options begin to dwindle. Human ingenuity creates a world that rushes toward ruin and chaos. As this time approaches, God releases more angelic intervention to protect His people and to promote His kingdom. Furthermore, for the past century, the church has been experiencing the renewal and restoration of the Pentecostal gifts.

Beginning at Azusa Street in the early twentieth century and continuing to this very day, a mighty outpouring of the Holy Spirit is sweeping across our world. Historians tell us that we are actually in the third wave of this worldwide move of the Spirit. Conversions to Christianity in the third world are reaching record numbers. Even the Islamic world is being powerfully impacted by the supernatural. Visions, dreams, and angels are appearing even where there is no missionary presence.

As churches and ministries embrace charismatic ministry, old divisions are falling away and kingdom unity is spreading worldwide. The last days' church must be kingdom oriented in order to release the supernatural, including miraculous angelic assistance.

KINGDOM MINISTRY

As we discuss the miracle ground that angels operate from, it is essential for us to know how to be in prime position to receive and activate their supernatural influence in our world. One of the main things to understand is how the kingdom of God works in relationship to us and the earth realm. As I have already pointed out, there are certain kingdom laws in the Word of God that angels abide by, and if we are to benefit from them as our allies, we need to abide by those laws as well. Our understanding of God's kingdom will help us understand the connection between the laws of the kingdom and our angelic allies.

According to Luke 17:21, the kingdom of God dwells within us. So if Jesus is Lord in our lives, then His kingdom has come through us. Yet we will have full access to it and its resources only once we are born again by the Spirit of God. (See John 3:5.) This access to kingdom resources requires a willingness to change (repent) and a submissive, broken spirit. (See Matthew 3:2; 6:33.) With the kingdom of God being present all around us through angelic miracles, old divisions between churches being broken down, and even conversions in Islamic countries, it is clear that we are living in a time of kingdom breakthrough.

But not only is the kingdom of God here now, it is also yet to come. Hebrews 2:8–9 says, "Yet now we do not see all things subject to him. But we see Jesus." We do not yet see all of the aspects and inner workings of God's kingdom, but its fullness is yet to come because we are still waiting for Jesus to return to the earth a second time. In John 18:36 Jesus confirms this by saying that the kingdom of God is "not of this world."

The kingdom breaks through into the "now" by the Holy Spirit. In the letters of Paul, he calls the baptism of the Holy Spirit a guarantee of the powers of the world to come in the here and now! Furthermore, the powers of the kingdom are released at our sealing and anointing. (See 2 Corinthians 1:21–22; Ephesians 1:14.) I am convinced that many Christians are children of the kingdom but are not sons! All who are saved are children, yet the rights of sonship, which include angels, miracles, signs, and wonders, belong to those who have been baptized in the Holy Spirit.

The Holy Spirit releases the power of the kingdom now! Angels are a part of that realm we call "the kingdom of heaven." When a church or a believer is willing to sell out to all God has, the angelic activity will increase exponentially! In a hurting, sad, and dirty world, we need this kingdom that is "righteousness and peace and joy in the Holy Spirit" (Rom. 14:17) to be activated.

Now that we have explored how we can be in position to receive and/or activate the kingdom of heaven with angelic ministry, let's look at some of the grounds upon which angels tread in order to impact the earth with kingdom power.

ANGELIC MINISTRY IN THE CHURCH

At Abba's House (Central Baptist Church, Chattanooga, Tennessee), where I have served for thirty years, we have moved from a traditional ministry to what some call charismatic. The transition began in 1989 and continues until this day. Since 1993 angel sightings, angelic singing, orbs of light, and bursts of fire have taken place. All of these manifestations occurred after I was baptized in the Holy Spirit and as the church moved into that realm. It is my belief that angelic ministry in today's kingdom church is similar to what took place in the New Testament church.

When we read the New Testament, we find its pages filled with angelic activity. When the church brings those who are lost to a saving knowledge of Jesus Christ, the angels join in the celebration and praise for their conversion. Scripture says that when the lost are found, "there is joy in the presence of the angels" (Luke 15:10). When the church gathers for worship, angels gather with us (Heb. 12:22). Angels exhibit a strong curiosity about believers' spiritual lives (1 Pet. 1:12). Undoubtedly because of their large number, their activity in the spiritual realm, and their presence among the members of the kingdom church, we are warned not to make the angels objects of our worship (Col. 2:18).

In his book *The Truth About Angels* Terry Law illustrates how angels are moved when we worship God. He shares several stories that tell of angelic activity in churches:[1]

> Sharon Abrams, a physician's wife who attends Agape Church, told of seeing two angels during a church

service. The angels were hovering over the congregation with their arms outstretched. They were light-skinned and had light-colored hair, and they stood seven or eight feet tall. Abrams wrote: "Their faces were broad with high cheekbones and beautiful smiles. They looked like men except they did not have beards. There was an innocence to their faces, and the joy of their expressions was wonderful. They did not wear shoes, but wore long white gowns with gold braid. I cannot remember exactly where the braid was located on the gowns. I knew they were in the service because of our praise and worship...because Jesus was being lifted up and adored. I sensed there were many more beings present in the auditorium, but I was only able to see those two."[2]

Marilyn Cappo of Louisville Covenant Church in Kentucky says she has seen angels on a number of occasions. She reported seeing three angels dancing on the roof of a house where a home group was meeting. One of them was playing something like a small harp, perhaps a lyre. Later, during a church morning worship service, she saw a nine-foot angel standing behind the worship leader. Most recently, she said she has seen two angels standing on the front platform of her church during several different services. She described them this way:

"They are a little over six feet tall and dressed in white. They do not speak but raise their wings when songs are sung of direct praise to the Father.

"They stand to the left of the pulpit, watching the congregation, and look at us expectantly. I have seen them off and on over a period of months and have prayed often to understand their purpose and mission at our church. One morning one of them walked over behind the pastor and spread his wings as our pastor was making declarative statements about God to us. The angels appear to be waiting for us to do something and always watch intently."

Patsy Burton of Wethersfield, Essex, in England,

wrote of hearing angels singing during a church service. She said the "clarity, pitch and harmony was absolutely incredible. In fact, there are no words to describe how they sounded."

In *Somewhere Angels,* one of the best books that I have found on angels, author Larry Libby wrote about a worship meeting in Alaska: "Outside, the winter wind moaned and hissed against the frosted church windows. But inside the little church, people were warm and happy and singing song after song of praise to God...something mysterious and wonderful happened that icy, starlit night. After one last praise song...people stopped singing. The musicians put down their instruments. But somehow, the singing kept going. Everyone heard it. The beautiful praise music kept rolling on and on for a little while, like a long, silvery echo."[3]

ANGELS AND KINGDOM LEADERSHIP

Furthermore, angels accompany those who serve in the fivefold ministry. Let's look carefully at this often-quoted but misunderstood scripture on angels: "Do not forget to entertain strangers, for thereby some have entertained angels unknowingly" (Heb. 13:2).

This verse, when viewed in context, concerns church authority and order. Believers are called to "remember those who rule over you" (Heb. 13:7). Note again the following mandate: "Obey your leaders and submit to them, for they watch over your souls . . . Let them do this with joy and not complaining, for that would not be profitable to you" (Heb. 13:17). The point is quite clear: angels accompany those who lead, speak the Word of God, teach faith, and watch for your souls, and they release profit or prosperity. When a believer refuses to submit to apostles, prophets, evangelists, pastors, and teachers, then the angels that accompany them are insulted and will not release blessing. Those who mock and make fun of men and women of God are blocking the ministry of angels.

The following story illustrates God's care for His chosen leaders through the intervention of angels. A missionary who came home for a short break shared this story at his home church in Michigan:

> While serving at a small field hospital in Africa, every two weeks I traveled by bicycle through the jungle to a nearby city for supplies. This was a journey of two days and required camping overnight at the halfway point. On one of these journeys, I arrived in the city where I planned to collect money from a bank, purchase medicine and supplies, and then begin my two-day journey back to the field hospital.
>
> Upon arrival in the city, I observed two men fighting, one of whom had been seriously injured. I treated him for his injuries and at the same time talked to him about the Lord. I then traveled two days, camping overnight, and arrived home without incident.
>
> Two weeks later I repeated my journey. Upon arriving in the city, I was approached by the young man I had treated. He told me that he had known I carried money and medicines. He said, "Some friends and I followed you into the jungle, knowing you would camp overnight. We planned to kill you and take your money and the drugs. But just as we were about to move into your camp, we saw that twenty-six armed guards surrounded you." At this, I laughed and said that I was certainly all alone in that jungle campsite.
>
> The young man pressed the point, however, and said, "No, sir, I was not the only person to see the guards; my friends also saw them and we all counted them. It was because of those guards that we were afraid and left you alone."
>
> At this point in the sermon, one of the men in the congregation jumped to his feet and interrupted the

missionary and asked if he could tell him the exact day this happened. The missionary told the congregation the date, and the man who interrupted told him this story.

"On the night of your incident in Africa, it was morning here and I was preparing to go play golf. I was about to putt when I felt the urge to pray for you. In fact, the urging of the Lord was so strong; I called some men in this church to meet with me here in the sanctuary to pray for you. Would all of those men who met with me on that day stand up?"

The men who had met together to pray that day stood up. The missionary wasn't concerned with who they were; he was too busy counting how many men he saw. There were twenty-six men.[4]

These stories make it clear that when we welcome the ministries of godly men and women, we entertain the angels who are assigned to them. Those accompanying angels are released in the community being visited by the guest; there they battle the ruling powers of the enemy and release the miracles of God. Only as we receive those whom God sets over us can we have the full ministry of the hosts at their disposal.

Even the business community can turn from loss to profit by welcoming God's servants and their angelic helpers. In the election of 2008, it is interesting that the financial downturn and loss of profit in America happened when the media and the Left mocked the faith of Sarah Palin. *Newsweek* mocked her charismatic expressions, and the media laughed. Angels of profit were insulted as this woman of God was not respected. You can mark the loss of profit in the stock market from the mocking of her charismatic faith. Angels were insulted and businesses failed. (See Hebrews 13:2, 17.)

ANGELS AND AWAKENING

The hosts of heaven can move on behalf of our Western nations again only if we respect the spiritual leaders God sends. When this happens, angels will come with fire to cleanse and to rekindle our spiritual lives. This will result in a release of supernatural power and resources. Hebrews 1:7 declares that angels are flames of fire. Pentecostal fire includes angelic fire released to do its powerful work in the earth. (Even our speaking in tongues is called "tongues of angels" by the Scriptures, as we see in 1 Corinthians 13:1.) As faith increases and the church operates in kingdom power, our angelic allies will help us take dominion in our communities and our nations. Let us activate our angels by making the kingdom of God our priority. God will order the angels into our dimension as we move in the power of the Holy Spirit.

Experiencing the Impossible

When I was a little child in kindergarten, I remember sitting in church with one of my friends, and we'd see angels fly around the sanctuary. This happened for several weeks. We would just sit there and talk about it back and forth together about how these angels we both could see were flying around. It was just so real. It was normal for us—we heard about angels in the Bible, and we would see them in the church.

So one day we shared about this with some adults in the church. Their response was, "You can't see angels. You're not able to see angels. That's impossible. You're making up stories."

And in that moment something happened, and all of a sudden a door shut off. A door came down and stopped all that from happening in my life. I never saw the angels in church again. I didn't see them anywhere, in fact, and I wasn't even aware of that realm any longer. And it was because people told me that it wasn't real.

What's amazing to me now as an adult is that the Bible doesn't say we are to come to God with faith like a sophisticated intellectual or like a well-educated individual. The Bible says we come to Him with faith like a little child (Luke 18:17).

Looking back on the situation, I realize that when I was a child, because I had heard what the Bible said and believed it, I was open to see in the spirit realm. It was so easy. I wasn't trying to make it happen. I wasn't striving. It just happened. My friend and I just saw the angels flying around in church. In fact, I didn't even ask to see the angelic. It just happened naturally.

But when other people got involved and began telling me what God can and cannot do, or will not do, the encounters stopped. When they told me what I should not be seeing, that shut it off for me.

It wasn't until years later when I was at Ruth Heflin's ministry that the supernatural realm was opened up again in my life. Ruth was a Pentecostal evangelist and revivalist. I was at her Calvary Pentecostal Campground when I began asking, "God, every kind of anointing, every kind of gift, every kind of spiritual blessing that is in this place that nobody else wants to receive, I want to receive it. Those things that are just lying dormant in this place, God, I just want to receive all of it."

I went to bed that night and had a dream. I saw three angels; they came to me, and when they did, I asked them their names. They told me their names, and in fact they told me they were my guardian angels and that they had been assigned over my life. They proceeded to tell me all the different things they had been assigned to do.

That marked the beginning, once again, of my being familiar with the angelic realm.

Since then God has taken me into the Word and shown me hundreds of scriptures detailing all kinds of encounters with the angelic realm, about how angels encounter mankind and how they interact with us.

God has even given me three keys for how I can activate the angelic realm in my life and how other believers can activate the angelic in their lives. It has been so powerful because, as I minister in that way, many people find themselves being activated in the angelic realm too.

The activation of the angelic realm is not for self-glory. It's not for self-promotion. It's not so we can say we're more spiritual than somebody else. The reason God sends angels to mankind, the reason God sends angels into the earth, is for interaction with mankind. It is for interaction with humanity so that the purposes of heaven can be released.

Ultimately, the purpose of the angelic realm interacting with mankind is so Jesus Christ will be glorified in the earth.

—JOSHUA MILLS, RECORDING ARTIST, AUTHOR, AND CONFERENCE SPEAKER WHO LEADS NEW WINE INTERNATIONAL

Chapter 17

FIVE BIBLICAL PRINCIPLES
THAT RELEASE ANGELS

By Terry Law

SSENTIALLY, ANGELS ARE agents of the government of God, the sovereign ruler of the universe (Isa. 46:8–11; Rom. 11:36; Eph. 1:11). Activities of angels in the Bible were directly related to God's sovereign plan. *Nothing done by any man controlled the angels.* Their primary motivation is obeying and serving God. However, men can do some things that activate angels, or put them in motion to act on their behalf.

In studying angels, I have discovered five biblical principles that seem to activate them to fulfill their role of serving God by serving His people. In other words, our actions seem to influence their actions. Those five principles are authority, sacrifice, prayer, giving in obedience (or alms), and praise and worship.

AUTHORITY

The first principle is obedience and submission to authority. When angels see us operating properly under authority, they are released to minister for us as the Holy Spirit wills.

The entire universe runs on the authority principle—including Satan's kingdom. The one place where authority is generally resisted is here on Earth.

As often as I have studied the subject of angels, I have been impressed time and again with the principle of authority as it relates to angels. God's angels operate under God's authority. Satan's angels operate under Satan's authority.

There is order in Satan's evil kingdom because it is an imitation of God's orderly, righteous kingdom. The most important point of all, however, as we consider just what the angelic hierarchy may signify, is that Jesus is high above them all. He has no equal and no superior.

He delegated His authority over evil spirits to the disciples even before He was crucified and resurrected. His example shows us how we are to walk in that delegated authority.

> Look, I give you authority to trample on serpents and scorpions, and over all the power of the enemy. And nothing shall by any means hurt you. Nevertheless do not rejoice that the spirits are subject to you, but rather rejoice that your names are written in heaven."
>
> —Luke 10:19–20

Evil spirits can tell whether a person is operating in the authority of God's Word. A biblical example involves seven sons of a Jewish priest named Sceva. They attempted to cast out an evil spirit in the name of Jesus "whom Paul preaches." But they were not born again, so they did not have the right to use the authority of Jesus, and the evil spirit overcame all seven of them (Acts 19:13–16). In fact, the possessed man tore the clothes off the seven men and chased them down the street.

The spirit's reply to these men was, "I know Jesus, and I know Paul, but who are you?" (Acts 19:15). You can almost hear the belligerence in the tone of that spirit. He would not obey anyone who did not have authority over him. This is a law in the spirit realm—the law of authority.

Author Neil Anderson says, "Spiritual authority is not a tug-of-war on a horizontal plane; it is a vertical chain of command." He wrote:

> Jesus Christ has all authority; He is on top.
>   We are underneath Jesus, because He gave His

> authority and power to His servants to be exercised in
> His name.
>
> And Satan and his demons? They're at the bottom,
> subject to the authority Christ has invested in us. They
> have no more right to rule your life than a buck private
> has to order a general to clean the latrine.[1]

If the church could get hold of this, the world would become a different place, even in the midst of the *cosmos diabolicus.*

Authority *carries* responsibility, and authority *follows* responsibility; it does not precede it. The Great Commission demonstrates this. Jesus said, *"All authority* in heaven and on earth has been given to me. Therefore go and make disciples of all nations" (Matt. 28:18–19, NIV, emphasis added). This is an incredible responsibility for the church. To get the job done, He has delegated His authority completely to the church. In other words, Jesus said, "Since I gave you the responsibility, you also have the authority of My name to do it."

If we don't take responsibility in this area, then our authority is canceled out. You may rule or govern by force, through some kind of power, but there is no authority behind it. Like the seven sons of Sceva, there is no point speaking to demons, much less principalities and powers, if you have not assumed responsibility for the lusts of your flesh.

Another element of authority is submission. Submission to authority is an act of obedience, but it is also a form of faithfulness.

If we want authority in the kingdom of God, we must learn first to be good followers and to submit to authority with the right attitude. God told the Israelites that if they were "willing and obedient" they would "eat the good of the land" (Isa. 1:19). Obedience under duress or with a reluctant heart is not true obedience.

In other words, if you want to operate in authority, you have to come under authority. That's because the levels of authority in the world are established by God. If you want to find out if you're under authority, see how you measure up to these seven guidelines. (These seven levels of authority are listed in order of supremacy.)

1. We must be obedient to the sovereign will of God. This is the highest level of authority. It is absolute and infallible.

2. We must be obedient to the veracity (truth) of God's Word. God's Word holds the position in the universe of veracious authority, with *veracious* meaning it is "always true."

3. We must not go against our own conscience. Some people's consciences will not permit them to do what other people can do. An angel of God would not ask you to go against your conscience—but an angel of light (one who presents a gospel other than what is found in God's Word) might.

4. We must obey the laws of the land and of our churches, as long as those directives do not conflict with those of the first three levels of authority. That's because all authority in the church and the world is delegated by Christ (Rom. 13:1). However, I am not advocating blind obedience to any law or man, but accepting civic and church authority as ordained and delegated by God.

   Attempts to coerce obedience by emotional or spiritual force—fear, shame, guilt, and other negative manipulative techniques—are abuses of authority. Tyrannical political systems, such as Nazism and Communism, are abusive authorities, not true representations of God-ordained authority.

5. We must honor stipulative authority, which is authority that is specified by agreement. An example of this kind of authority is parties signing a contract that is legally binding.

6. We must honor tradition if it has not become abusive or is not in conflict with other levels of authority. For example, tradition is wrong when it is given higher authority than the Word of God (Matt. 15:3–6).

7. We must honor the authority of others, which stems from their talents, abilities, or skills. This is called functional authority, and, again, its origin is in God. We go to a doctor when we're sick—not a mechanic.[2]

Authority and our words

The authority of our words depends on whether or not we obey or submit to the levels of authority over us. Let's compare the difference between Mary's words of faith and Zacharias's words of doubt when they had visits from the angel Gabriel. It must have been difficult for both of them to believe Gabriel; Zacharias was too old to have a child, and Mary was a virgin.

Zacharias asked a question that was full of doubt—he almost seemed to be asking for a sign that what Gabriel said would really happen (Luke 1:18). "How shall I know this? For I am an old man and my wife well advanced in years," he said. Gabriel acted quickly to stop Zacharias's words of unbelief (Luke 1:20). Zacharias was struck dumb and could not speak until John was born. He got his sign, but it probably wasn't the kind he wanted. Angels are sensitive to what we say. It appears our words of faith or doubt can "activate" or "deactivate" them.

Mary *submitted* to the authority of God's Word and said, "May it be unto me according to your word" (Luke 1:38). I believe she became pregnant at that very moment. Her faith activated the Word of God, which immediately became flesh inside of her. Her submission to authority became faith that resulted in the conception of Jesus, the Son of God, in her womb. Her response is one of the most powerful faith statements in the Bible.

Jesus taught that we are redeemed, justified, or made righteous by our words, and we are also condemned by our words (Matt.

12:37). When we are sensitive to God, it is easy to discern the oppressive atmosphere created by words of doubt and unbelief.

Angels are watching the church.

Through Jesus, the church has been raised higher than the angels. We are of the family of God and seated at the right hand of the throne of God with Jesus. What a position of authority this gives to the church! Jesus delegated His authority to the church, and because angels understand authority, they are watching to see what we do with that authority.

When Christians get the revelation of their position in Christ, when they stand against the enemy in the power of the name of Jesus, recognizing the authority God has given to the church, angels understand that authority. If our desire is to see God's will done on earth, and we are under authority, angels will flow with us.

SACRIFICE

Sacrificing in any area out of love for God is the second principle that I believe activates angels. It shows a wholeheartedness toward God that brings a response. Sacrifice is actually closely related to praise and worship.

I wrote about sacrifice in one of my earlier books:

> God required that Cain and Abel bring a sacrifice to Him. Abel offered the animal sacrifice that was pleasing to the Lord (a substitution of a living being for himself). Cain offered the Lord the first part of his harvest, the fruit of the ground, but this was unacceptable (involving no sacrifice). As a result, Cain killed Abel out of jealousy.
>
> Abraham and David clearly understood the principle of sacrifice. Abraham was willing to sacrifice his son Isaac to the Lord on Mount Moriah. An angel appeared as Abraham raised his knife, prepared to take Isaac's life. David had to offer a sacrifice to God on the threshing floor of Ornan the Jebusite in order to stop the death

angel whose sword was stretched over Jerusalem to destroy it.[3]

You may be wondering why God requires sacrifice. From the time Adam and Eve disobeyed, man has been the creature separated from the Creator by sin. The only way to approach God's holiness was through the substitutionary death of a living creature. The penalty for disobedience, required of all the human race after Adam fell, was death (Gen. 2:17). Until Jesus died vicariously once and for all, there had to be a death. Blood is a proof of such death, because the life is in the blood (Deut. 12:23). Animal sacrifice was a substitution—a merciful token of the one-time sacrifice of Jesus yet to come.

Why did David refuse to take the threshing floor of Ornan (Araunah) as a gift, but insist on paying full price for it before he made sacrifice to God (2 Sam. 24:18–25; 1 Chron. 21:17–30; 2 Chron. 3:1)? David knew it was not a real offering unless it had cost him something. Human nature (our souls) would far prefer to praise God when things are going well, but to grumble and complain when they are not!

We tend to say, "God, what have You done for me lately?" That attitude will not activate angels on our behalf. Sacrificial worship provides a legal right for the angels to ascend and descend to and from God's throne bringing help to the saints. Gideon and Manoah and his wife offered sacrifices while they were being visited by angels, and the angels returned to heaven while the sacrifices burned (Judg. 6:21; 13:20). Most churches have praise and worship services, but most do not really understand what they are doing.

When Gabriel appeared to Zacharias to announce the birth of John the Baptist, it was while the priest was offering a sacrifice of incense to the Lord. Incense is a symbol of pure worship. In other words, Zacharias's sacrifice unto the Lord brought the angel to him with an answer to his lifelong prayer for a son.

I have found that if I can lead people into a sacrifice of praise, something about that brings angelic involvement. This is especially true of those who are sick and suffering.

PRAYER—THE WORD OF GOD ON OUR LIPS

The third principle that activates angels is prayer, especially praying God's Word back to Him. There is no question that prayer activates angels on our behalf. Moses's prayers of repentance on behalf of the Israelites saved them from destruction several times (Num. 14:11–21; 21:5–9; and others). Abraham's intercession on behalf of Lot and his family activated angels to rescue them (Gen. 18:17–33). Those are two of many biblical examples.

The primary way to renew our minds so that any thoughts dropped in by evil spirits cannot find a lodging place is to meditate on the Bible. I have found that something special happens in the angelic kingdom when Christians speak God's Word in the midst of contrary circumstances. It somehow releases the angelic world to work alongside us.

Our prayers are much more effective when we pray God's Word back to Him. That allows us to get in agreement with Him instead of wasting time and energy imploring Him to get in agreement with us. Many times we tend to pray the problem and talk about the problem so much that we finally operate in "negative faith"—faith that something bad is going to happen or is happening. Problems do not activate angels. God's Word activates angels.

Promises from God's Word bring provisions, including the assistance of angels if that is needed. Someone has said there are seven thousand promises in the Bible. God does not want to hear the problem. He wants to hear the promise that fixes the problem. He wants to hear us praise Him in advance for that promise. He honors prayer that costs us something.

Remember, prayer by the church brought an angel to Peter in prison. Prayer brought an angel to shut the mouths of lions for Daniel. Faith words (prayer) by the three Hebrew children brought the fourth man into the fiery furnace.

GIVING IN OBEDIENCE

The fourth principle that activates angels involves giving to God's work, God's people, or to the poor and needy. Something about money and its use by the church touches the world of angels. Sacrificial giving activates angels as much as sacrificial praise. Evil spirits are trying today to hinder giving by God's people.

Cornelius, the first Gentile to be filled with the Holy Spirit, was a giver. The angel told him his prayers and his alms (money) had come up as a memorial before God (Acts 10:3).

When Satan became "god of this world" (2 Cor. 4:4), the finances of the world also passed under Satan's authority. The world economic system is Satan's system, his way of handling trade and money, not God's.

However, through the work Jesus did on the cross, the authority over the world's resources once again became God's. Because God has given us the responsibility to reach the world, He also has given us the authority to get the job done. Through the delegation of that authority, the church should be taking dominion over the silver and gold through biblical principles. Our stewardship in finance demonstrates probably more than anything else whether we have come under God's authority. The angels are aware of how we handle our money.

Kenneth Hagin Sr. used to say that when the Lord showed him the ministry of angels, it included help with finances. He was given these three steps to activate angelic help:

1. Claim what you need.

2. Tell the devil to take his hands off your money or resources.

3. Tell the ministering angels to go forth and bring you what is needed.

Hagin said the angels of the Lord are waiting for the church to give orders according to the Word of God and under the direction of the Holy Spirit.

Willie George, pastor of Church on the Move in Tulsa, Oklahoma, also believes very firmly that angels are involved with finances on behalf of the children of God.

The principle of giving in obedience was demonstrated to me when I was a very young pastor. This incident changed the course of my entire life. In 1967, I pastored a little church in Hatton, Saskatchewan, on the prairies of western Canada. My father was pastor of a larger church in Medicine Hat, Alberta, fifty miles away. My congregation numbered about twenty-five; it was an event when thirty people showed up for a meeting!

Obviously, a congregation this size could not pay me a full salary, so I supplemented my income by working with a local farmer, Ed Stahl. Ed was a successful farmer with a herd of five hundred pure-bred Herefords running on thirteen square miles of fairly barren, dry prairie land. Finding water for their stock was one of the biggest problems for area ranchers and farmers.

However, Ed was a very unusual man and one of the most godly, honest men I have ever known. He did not walk when he worked—he trotted; all day long he prayed and talked to the Lord. One night, in a vision, God showed him where pockets of water form on the prairies. After that, Ed found water everywhere he dug for it.

He also had large wheat and hay operations, and my work included branding cattle in the spring and riding a tractor sowing wheat seed. During the summer, I spent long periods baling hay, hauling the heavy hay bales, and stacking them in the yard. Then, in the fall, I rode the combine and helped with the wheat harvest.

In the late summer of 1967, I heard that Oral Roberts was coming to Edmonton, Alberta, for a healing crusade. Edmonton is about three hundred fifty miles north of Medicine Hat, and I got permission from Ed to take off work to attend one of the meetings. I had never seen Oral Roberts in person and did not know very much about his ministry.

I made the trip during the day. That night Roberts preached and prayed for the sick, which I watched intently, then I left for the parking lot.

In the lobby, I passed a large table with books and tapes and another table with literature promoting a school just started in Tulsa, Oklahoma, named Oral Roberts University. I paused at the book table for a moment, then picked up one of the brochures about the university.

As I picked it up, I had an overwhelming inner awareness that I was to attend ORU. I felt the call of God so strongly that I literally groaned. The last thing I wanted to do was go to school two thousand miles away! The biggest problem would be tuition and other expenses. My weekly salary was only about fifty dollars. There was no way I would be able to save the money. Besides that, like many other young preachers, I felt I was ready to "turn the world upside down" with the Bible school education I already had!

During the long trip home tears rolled down my cheeks as this strong call from God echoed inside me. For the next three months I wrestled with this, not telling anyone else about it, not even my father or mother. I did not mention it to Ed as we worked side by side during those three months. However, after three months of struggling every night with this call and my uncertainty about finances, I finally gave up.

One night, I said to the Lord, "All right! I'll go to Tulsa!"

The next day Ed and I were working together digging holes for fence posts. This is hard, back-breaking work, and I paused for a moment with a posthole augur in my hand and with sweat rolling down my forehead. Ed was standing at the back of a half-ton pickup truck pulling fence posts out of the truck bed to drop into the holes I dug.

I said, "Ed, I made a major decision last night. I believe the Lord has called me to attend Oral Roberts University, and I have made up my mind. I don't know how yet, but I'm going to go."

Tears came into his eyes so suddenly that I thought he had dropped a post on his toe.

He said, "Get in the truck. I want to show you something."

So I jumped in, and we traveled a couple of miles across the prairie up to the top of a hill.

"Do you see that spot over there?" he asked. "Three months ago I was working in the field with one of the bulls when suddenly an angel of the Lord stood before me.

"The light was so bright I didn't dare look at him, and I fell on my knees. The angel spoke to me and said, 'Terry Law is going to make a decision. He is going to go to Oral Roberts University in Tulsa. When he makes that decision, God the Father wants you to cover the financial obligations of his university education. You are to pay the bills and make sure everything is taken care of.'"

It was my turn for tears to well up in my eyes. The decision I had struggled with, which looked so impossible, had been taken care of by the Lord even while He was calling me to go. Ed was faithful to the command of the Lord and covered my entire university education.

Since my graduation, I have seen literally hundreds of thousands of people make decisions for Jesus Christ in my missionary travels around the world. I believe that Ed Stahl has a share in every one of those people because he was obedient to the words of the angel sent by God.

Angels Released While Giving

One of the funniest times I have encountered angels was in the form of wind. It was also probably the most intense experience I have had.

It happened when my husband, Robert John, and I were just engaged and decided to tithe together jointly for the first time. Though we were not married, we decided we would make our first tithe, our first gift, together. It happened on a supernormal day. We were at his mom's house, in the basement working at the computer. We decided to give to a ministry online, and it was pretty routine. We went to the ministry's website, clicked "Donate Now," and literally in that very moment it was as if somebody dropped fans into the room. It was as if suddenly all these high-powered fans started blowing.

It was a really intense encounter with the wind of heaven!

These winds were ripping through the room, and instantly we felt filled and refreshed with the Holy Spirit and God's joy. There was an intense sense of God's pleasure with our unity, our unity in giving and our unity in giving to the kingdom. Because God loves it all—He loves our unity, He loves giving, and He definitely loved what the ministry that we gave to was doing. He loved where our first tithe was going.

We were experiencing the joy and pleasure of the Lord. But there was also a sense that something was activated by that act of giving. We know from the Word that angels are dispatched on assignment. God gives angels assignments, and we had a sense that angels were being dispatched in that moment. There was a connection to this action we had just taken as a couple, and now the angels were going to carry out the assignment on our behalf.

And we know from the Bible that there is a principle of sowing and reaping. We weren't sowing just for a reaping, just for a release; we were doing it because we love God and we love to give. But what unfolded in the next couple of weeks was—I want to call it *paranormal* because it was not normal at all.

Shortly after this experience I went to speak at a conference, and it was just nine days before we were to get married. And for Robert John and I, even our wedding was a step of faith. We were going to be newlyweds, and we were paying for the entire wedding ourselves. We were simply trusting God to cover the bills.

So at this conference, completely unprompted, one of the other speakers gets up and announces that I am getting married in nine days. It was just a fun moment. But afterward a couple who had traveled there all the way from Ireland came up to me and said, "Faytene, while that minister was sharing about you getting married, we really felt like we wanted to sow into the beginning of this new phase in life for you and your husband. If we want to make out a check, where would we make it out, who would we make it out to?"

I was very humbled and had no idea what they were going to do, but I gave them my bank information, and they ended up wiring ten thousand dollars into our new beginning. We were, like, "*Whoa!* This is wild!"

It was the blessing of our Father in heaven who wanted to bless us at the beginning of our new phase.

Looking back, I believe there was something dispatched in the spirit realm through that joint act of giving, that first tithe we made as a couple. For me the manifestation of the wind is a confirmation of that. It was a fruit of the Father's goodness being poured out on us. We were able not only to get married but also to get married with our entire wedding completely paid for. I believe the angels were involved in administrating that blessing!

—Faytene Grasseschi, pioneering director of TheCRY prayer movement

PRAISE AND WORSHIP

The fifth principle that seems to activate angels is praise and worship of God. As I mentioned in chapter fourteen, before he fell, I believe Satan led the angelic hosts in praise and worship to the Father. He was heaven's choir director. Music was not created as a tool—even for evangelism—although God does use it that way. Music was originally ordained for one purpose—to worship the Father.

When Lucifer took his eyes off God and focused them on his own beauty and brilliance, something happened inside him. He became filled with pride. He began to desire worship for himself instead of giving and leading worship to God.

Satan's primary drive today is still to get worship for himself in any way that he can. His temptation of Jesus was designed to get the Lord to worship him! As theologian Lewis Chafer wrote, one can hardly think of a more audacious, arrogant, conceited act. He failed with Jesus, who told him it was written that only God shall be worshipped and served.[4]

Satan's challenge concerning Job was one of the greatest insults he has ever given God.[5] He implied that God really cannot be loved for Himself, but only for what He does for people or for what He gives them. Satan was saying God has to bribe people to serve Him. No wonder the Lord allowed Job to be tested! God knew what Satan was saying could be proven false. He knew Job's heart.

Jesus asked the same thing of the multitudes who followed Him after the miracle of the loaves and fishes. In effect, He said, "Are you following Me because of who I am, or because of what I can do for you?" (See John 6:26–27.)

True worship comes out of love and reverence, not fear, coercion, or a desire to be better off. This is what Satan has never understood. Judson Cornwall wrote:

> Satan is still far more interested in worship than in sin. He is more likely to be in church than in the worst den of iniquity in any area. This fallen angel would rather pervert a person's worship than corrupt his morals, for he knows that if he can pervert our worship, we will corrupt our morals.[6]

Satan is a very religious being who desires and probably needs praise and worship. His goal is far less to destroy mankind than it is to receive worship from those created to worship God. He knows the power that praise and worship generate in the spiritual realm. He knows that praise and worship generate healing and spiritual breakthrough. If Satan cannot subvert it to attention on himself, he tries to kill praise and worship altogether by turning it into ritualistic religion.

Today, Satan is working on people, whispering in the ears of anyone who appears to have talent, promising them popularity and prosperity. Many top music groups today actually give Satan the credit for the lyrics they "receive" while high on drugs. Some groups perform songs seeking sympathy and worship for Satan. Christians who chant Satan's name or sing choruses about him as a part of spiritual warfare do not realize it, but he counts that as worship, not warfare.

Music played an incredibly important role in the Bible. There are more than eight hundred references to music, while hell is only mentioned seventy times. Our church services would be more productive in spiritual terms if we could learn that music is not a preliminary to the message, nor an icebreaker to get people warmed up. The song service is the protocol that God designed for the body of Christ to come into His presence.

Protocol is the procedure to be followed in approaching royalty and dignitaries on earth, a "code of ceremonial forms." When we were invited to the Vatican, a monsignor took me aside and instructed me on the proper protocol. He said, "Terry, you are a Protestant leader. When a Protestant meets the pope, he does not respond to him as a Roman Catholic would. I want to tell you the proper phrases so that you will feel comfortable. You will not feel as if you are compromising your beliefs, or fear that you might show disrespect to a head of state."

I was taught protocol because addressing a cardinal, as we knew him first in Poland, and addressing the pope require different approaches. When I met Pope John Paul II, I felt as comfortable talking with him as I had when he was a cardinal. I knew the proper way to approach him.

The highest office in the universe is God the Father. If earthly officials require a certain protocol to approach them with respect, how much more should we feel that way about the Creator? Visitors usually bring gifts to heads of state. My group and I also took gifts to the pope: a cowboy hat from Oklahoma, among other things.

The psalmist David indicated that the first step in the protocol of approaching God is thanksgiving. In Psalm 100:4, David wrote that we should enter into His gates with thanksgiving. The next step is to enter His courts with praise. Using the pattern of the tabernacle, David was saying, "Come into the outer court of God with thanksgiving and into the holy place with praise."

Thanksgiving in the Bible is retelling what God had already done for people. How often God's children come to Him with shopping lists of what we need or want Him to do. How seldom do we come with a "thanksgiving list" from the past. However, giving thanks for past blessings is one of the greatest faith builders that I know.

In the story of Jehoshaphat, king of Judah, we see an example of protocol in approaching God (2 Chron. 20:1–29). Jehoshaphat's heart was filled with fear when he found that three kings had invaded his territory with their armies.

The king first went to the Lord with thanksgiving. He reminded him of His greatness and of what He had done for the Israelites previously (2 Chron. 20:5–12). Then he essentially asked God to do it again.

A plan given to Judah by God through a young prophet was to send the Levites, the priests, out ahead of the army singing and praising the Lord for His mercy that endures forever. A group of singers moving toward the enemy ahead of the soldiers would have been afraid, but they obeyed in the face of fear. They brought gifts to God of sacrificial praise, and God "set ambushes" (2 Chron. 20:22). The result was that the three armies—Moab, Ammon, and Mount Seir—turned on one another and destroyed one another.

As I read this one day, the word *ambushes* caught my attention. I began to trace it through the Bible. I saw that God consistently uses angels to set up ambushes. Some of these were for individuals such as Balaam. Others were *for* Israel and Judah. Still other ambushes of God were *against* Israel and Judah when the nations departed from following God's ways.

Perhaps the angels sang along with Jehoshaphat's priests. As you've read earlier in the book, there have been many reports of people seeing angels during praise and worship services. Other people have heard angels singing along with the congregation. So, angels may not only watch us worshipping, but also join in.

Angels Increasing Finances

Once we ministered in a place called Maripasoula in French Guiana. We took a seaplane deep into the jungle, into a truly primitive area, where there was a huge tree so contorted I'd never seen anything like it. It looked haunted.

I asked the pastor I was with, "What is that?" He told me it was a demonic tree. It was where the native people worshipped—they would worship the tree and channel demons that used the tree like an antenna.

"That is so strange!" I said.

But the pastor told me, "Do not talk against that tree. If you do, they will kill you."

I wondered what I should do. So I preached on the cross—the only tree that can bring salvation! Since these people worshipped the contorted tree for protection, health, prosperity, and whatever else, I preached that there is a greater tree: the cross.

As I preached, the power of God came, and the angels came and the glory came. Then, in the middle of the meeting, the Lord told me to have the people give an offering. I questioned that because these were very poor people. I told the Lord I had come there to help them and that they didn't have anything to give. They didn't even have shoes—nothing.

But the Lord told me, "Take up an offering. Have them give. You do not understand; giving is worship. These people are worshipping the demonic entities and giving them food and gold and all sorts of things. If you have them give now, it will shift their worship. It will bring down My glory and the angels because worship opens the heavens—just like when Elijah put the sacrifice on the altar."

So I did. I took up an offering, knowing that one-fourth of the room was witches and sorcerers. And the people gave. And when they started giving, mass deliverance began to occur. Suddenly, during the actual offering, healings, signs, and wonders broke out. It was amazing. One-fourth of the town was saved at that service.

After that night, after taking the offering in the midst of the angelic and the glory, money has been pouring in from all over the place into that village, the pastor told us. Before we came, they had nothing—no money, nothing. Now they have exploded financially. People from everywhere are simply compelled to bless them and help them.

—DAVID HERZOG, AUTHOR AND FOUNDER WITH HIS WIFE, STEPHANIE, OF DAVID HERZOG MINISTRIES

Chapter 18

FIVE THINGS THAT HINDER
ANGELIC ACTIVITY

By Perry Stone

E KNOW FROM Ephesians 4:30 that it is possible to grieve the Holy Spirit. Just as it is possible to grieve the Holy Spirit, it is also possible to grieve the Father. God was grieved by the wanderings and disobedience of the children of Israel as they journeyed toward the Promised Land. In Psalm 95 we are warned:

> Do not harden your hearts, as in the rebellion,
> As in the day of trial in the wilderness,
> When your fathers tested Me;
> They tried Me, though they saw My work.
> For forty years I was grieved with that generation,
> And said, "It is a people who go astray in their hearts,
> And they do not know My ways."
> So I swore in My wrath,
> "They shall not enter My rest."
> —PSALM 95:8–11, NKJV

It is also possible to grieve the heart of Jesus. Several times in the New Testament, Jesus rebuked the disciples for their unbelief. He even wept at the tomb of Lazarus, not because Lazarus had died, but because He knew He was going to raise him from the dead. He wept because of the unbelief of the people around Him. (See John 11.)

Let's carry this a step further. If we can grieve the Holy Spirit, the Father, and Jesus Christ, then it is possible also to offend or grieve the angel of the Lord. In this chapter, we are going to not only find out that it is possible to do this, but we will also learn five things that grieve the angel of the Lord.

Angelic messengers are special messengers from God— appointed by God Himself. We learned earlier that angels are often called *ministering spirits* (Ps. 104:4). They go forth according to the purposes of God to complete a specific work, task, or assignment from the Lord.

WHAT HAPPENS WHEN YOU OFFEND YOUR ANGEL?

Before we discuss the five things that can offend an angel, let's see what happens when an angel is offended. There is a story in the Bible that gives us a graphic look at this. In 1 Chronicles 21:1 we are told, "Now Satan stood up against Israel, and moved David to number Israel." David sent his commander, Joab, throughout the land to find out how many people they had.

In Exodus 30:11–12 we see that God had given clear instructions to Moses that whenever a census was taken of the people of Israel, every man in Israel was supposed to pay half a shekel unto the Lord as a ransom for his soul, or as the price of redemption. David numbered the people, but he did not pay the half shekel. David's disobedience angered God, so God sent a plague, and seventy thousand men died as a result of the plague (1 Chron. 21:14).

God sent an angel to destroy Jerusalem, the city of David, which is located on what is known today as Mount Moriah. When King David saw the destruction that God was bringing to Jerusalem, he realized that God was sending judgment because of his sin. As he looked up from where he stood on the slopes of Mount Moriah, he "saw the angel of the LORD standing between earth and heaven, having in his hand a drawn sword stretched out over Jerusalem" (1 Chron. 21:16, NKJV). Immediately, David and all the elders clothed themselves in sackcloth and fell on their faces in repentance. The Lord "looked and relented of the disaster, and said to the angel who was destroying, 'It is enough; now restrain your hand'" (v. 15, NKJV).

David ran to the top of the mountain and bought a threshing floor site from Ornan the Jebusite so that he could erect an altar to the Lord. We discover that Ornan had also seen the angel of the Lord, and in great fear he offered to give David everything he had—land and all. But David would not take it without paying full price for it.

It was there that David "built there an altar to the LORD, and offered burnt offerings and peace offerings, and called on the LORD; and He answered him from heaven by fire on the altar of burnt offering" (v. 26, NKJV).

This is an example of a man willfully choosing to disobey God and of an angel becoming angry. That very mountain is the place where Abraham also built an altar and willingly offered to sacrifice his son, Isaac, in obedience to God. And, of course, Mount Moriah is the place where Jesus, the Son of the living God, was crucified and paid the price of our redemption.

THE ANGEL OF THE LORD AS THE PREINCARNATE JESUS

There is a very important scripture about an angel in Exodus 23:

> Behold, I send an Angel before you to keep you in the way and to bring you into the place which I have prepared. Beware of Him and obey His voice; do not provoke Him, for He will not pardon your transgressions; for My name is in Him. But if you indeed obey His voice and do all that I speak, then I will be an enemy to your enemies and an adversary to your adversaries. For My Angel will go before you.
> —EXODUS 23:20–23, NKJV

Here is the setting: The children of Israel were coming out of the bondage of Egypt and needed to know the direction they were to take in the wilderness. There were no road maps, signs, or GPS navigational systems to lead them. God had told them that He would not lead them through the land of the Philistines along the Sea: "'Lest perhaps the people change their minds when they see war, and return to Egypt.' So God led the people around by way of the wilderness of the Red Sea" (Exod. 13:17–18, NKJV). Instead, God said that He would lead the people by way of the wilderness.

I used to get frustrated with the Israelites who complained and bickered so much during the years they spent wandering around the wilderness. But over the years, however, I've driven with many tour buses through that same wilderness, and believe me, I now understand. The heat pouring off the rocks and sand is intolerable; it truly is a "no-man's-land."

But God had already determined a way of leading them out and giving them direction. He was going to send an angel before them to keep them on the right path and to bring them to the land He had promised to them.

It is important to note that in Exodus 23:20 God said He was sending "an Angel" to guide them. A few verses later, God changes it to say, "My Angel" (v. 23). God gave one very unusual clue about this angel when He said, "My name is in Him" (v. 21). God had many names, including *El Shaddai, El-Elyon, Adonai,* and *El,* which is an Old Testament root name for *God* (Deut. 5:9). The two angels most recognized in the Bible are Gabriel and Michael— both names containing *el,* the name of God! In Exodus 6:3, God revealed Himself as *Yahweh,* appearing in Hebrew as four letters— *YHVH*—which is called the *tetragrammaton.* Many Jews still today will not try to pronounce that name because they consider it too sacred to speak aloud. When they write it, they often leave the word blank or write the name as "G-D." This is a special angel, not a normal fighting prince or fighting angel. The Israelites were told, "Beware of Him and obey His voice; do not provoke Him, for He will not pardon your transgressions" (Exod. 23:21, NKJV). This angel had to be something more than a regular angel. But it was not God, for only God can forgive sins, and this angel could not.

Many theologians believe this angel was the preincarnate Jesus. Preincarnate simply means existence prior to His incarnation, or birth. There are several other places in the Old Testament where Jesus is seen in His preincarnate state as the angel of the Lord:

- After Hagar became pregnant with Ishmael and was sent out away from the camp of Abraham, we see that "the Angel of the LORD found her by a spring of water in the wilderness, by the spring on the way to Shur" (Gen. 16:7, NKJV).

- Later when Abraham sent Hagar and Ishmael away at the insistence of Sarah, Hagar went a short distance into the wilderness and fell to the ground, weeping about her situation. Then we see that "the angel of God called to Hagar out of heaven" and ministered to her, giving her a promise that God would make of Ishmael a great nation (Gen. 21:17–19).

- The angel of the Lord wrestled with Jacob (Gen. 32:24–30).

- The angel of the Lord spoke to Moses out of the burning bush (Exod. 3:1–14).

- The angel of the Lord stood in the way of Balaam and caused his donkey to speak (Num. 22:22–38).

- The angel of the Lord, as the captain of the host of the Lord, instructed Joshua to destroy Jericho (Josh. 5:13–6:5).

- The angel of the Lord called Gideon to lead the Israelites against the Midianites (Judg. 6:11–24).

- The angel of the Lord was the fourth man in the fire with Shadrach, Meshach, and Abed-nego (Dan. 3:28).

Was it Christ Himself who came down as the angel of the Lord? I believe that is more than likely. Usually when either

Michael the archangel or Gabriel the messenger of God appeared in the Bible, they were named. (See Daniel 10:13; Luke 1:19, 26; Jude 9; Revelation 12:7.)

This angel who is instructed to lead the Israelites to the Promised Land is never mentioned by name. His name is secret. I believe that it was Jesus Christ in preincarnate form as the angel of the Lord who ministered to these Old Testament Bible characters. The "Angel of the LORD" never appears in the New Testament after the birth of Christ.

"Do Not Provoke Him"

The people of Israel were told not to provoke the angel of the Lord. If they did, they would be in serious trouble. *Provoke* means to grieve greatly or to vex a person. This is exactly what the Israelites did with their unbelief, bickering, and complaining. As a result, serious trouble came, and came swiftly.

- They complained about the long walk through the wilderness:

  Now when the people complained, it displeased the LORD; for the LORD heard it, and His anger was aroused. So the fire of the LORD burned among them, and consumed some in the outskirts of the camp. Then the people cried out to Moses, and when Moses prayed to the LORD, the fire was quenched. So he called the name of the place Taberah, because the fire of the LORD had burned among them.
  —Numbers 11:1–3, nkjv

- They complained about Moses's Ethiopian wife:

  Then Miriam and Aaron spoke against Moses because of the Ethiopian woman whom he had married; for he had married an Ethiopian woman...So the anger of the LORD was aroused against them, and He departed. And

when the cloud departed from above the tabernacle, suddenly Miriam became leprous, as white as snow.
—NUMBERS 12:1, 9–10, NKJV

• They complained about the giants in the land:

There we saw the giants (the descendants of Anak came from the giants); and we were like grasshoppers in our own sight, and so we were in their sight.
—NUMBERS 13:33, NKJV

If this kind of complaining would grieve God in the Old Testament, I guarantee you that it will grieve God in the New Testament church of today. That's one of the things we have to be careful about.

Forty years after they left Egypt, the angel of the Lord had brought them to the edge of the Promised Land. As Joshua stood at the edge of the Promised Land, "a Man stood opposite him with His sword drawn in His hand" (Josh. 5:13, NKJV). Joshua approached the man and asked, "Are You for us or for our adversaries?"

The man responded, "As captain of the host of the LORD am I now come" (v. 14, KJV). The Hebrew word used for "host" indicates a mass of people organized for war—an army. One of the names of God, used in Romans 9:29, is "The Lord of Sabaoth." It is the same word as *host* and is the name for an army. I believe that the captain of the host of the Lord standing before Joshua was none other than the angel of the Lord who had led Moses and the children of Israel through the wilderness for forty years. Now the cloud was gone, and the angel of the Lord, the preincarnate Christ, was prepared to lead Joshua and the people into the Promised Land.

FIVE THINGS THAT OFFEND THE ANGELS OF THE LORD

The children of Israel provoked the angel of the Lord to anger, or offended him by their actions over and over again on the journey to the Promised Land. As a result, they wandered for forty long, unnecessary years. Even after they took possession of the land, they continued to offend God with their actions, and as a result, they were repeatedly harassed, defeated, and taken captive by their enemies.

It is important to learn what offends the angels God has assigned to protect our lives and to direct us in the paths of the Lord for our lives. There are five things that we can discover that will bring offense to the angels watching over us:

1. Negative words or wrong speaking will offend the angels.

Your negative words or wrong speaking can offend your angel. Psalm 103:20 (NKJV) says:

> Bless the LORD, you His angels,
> Who excel in strength, who do His word,
> Heeding the voice of His word.

The angels of the Lord are commissioned to listen to and be obedient to the voice of His Word. The Word of God moves the angels into action. First Peter 1:12 tells us that angels desire to look into the truth of the gospel and what it means. They crave knowledge about the preaching of the gospel and desire an understanding of God's Word about the blood of Jesus and its power to redeem mankind.

We learn in Hebrews 2:2 that "the word spoken through angels proved steadfast" (NKJV). God's Word tells us that the Law of God was given on Mount Sinai with ten thousand angels present (Deut. 33:2). The Word of God moves angels into action. I believe that in the same way, man's disobedience to the Word of God will offend the angels and cause them to withhold their protection.

In the time of Israel's release from the bondage of Egypt, Pharaoh was judged by how he treated the Israelite people. He came against the word of God given to him by Moses, and as a result, plagues were released against Egypt.

When the Hebrew people began to speak against God in the

wilderness, difficulties began to rise against them, including plagues and disease. (See related sidebar for examples.)

Plagues Brought on by Israelites' Complaints

- They began to misuse their tongue, and fire came into the camp and destroyed them (Num. 11:1).
- When the people began to lust after the rich foods they had eaten in Egypt and complained and wept for meat to eat, the Lord sent quail. But as judgment for their disobedience and misuse of their tongues, sickness immediately fell upon them from eating the quail (Num. 11:4–35).
- When Miriam and Aaron misused their tongues to complain about the Ethiopian woman Moses had married, the anger of the Lord was kindled against them, and a plague of leprosy came upon Miriam (Num. 12:1–16).
- When the ten spies returned with reports of "giants in the land" too powerful to overcome, the people began complaining against Moses and the Lord for bringing them to a land filled with enemies, and they wanted to choose another leader. However, Caleb and Joshua reported that they were well able to overcome, and begged them to stop their complaining and to trust God's leading. The people wanted to stone Caleb and Joshua instead. As a result, God told Moses that the entire generation who complained would die without ever being allowed to enter the Promised Land (Num. 13:31–33; 14:1–35).

- When Korah and his company of men challenged the authority and leadership of Moses and Aaron and tried to assume spiritual leadership of the children of Israel, God became angry and caused an earthquake to open the ground under the tents of Korah and all his followers, and they were destroyed in the pit (Num. 16:1–40).

- The day after God destroyed Korah and his company, the people of Israel again complained to Moses, saying that he had killed the people of the Lord. In anger, God caused a plague to immediately begin to kill off the Israelites. Moses and Aaron quickly began to intercede for the people and wave an offering of incense over the people to God, and in response, God stopped the plague—but 14,700 people died as a result of the judgment of God (Num. 16:41–50).

- After a great victory over the Canaanites, the people began a journey through Edom and again complained to Moses and God for having to travel in the heat of the desert without their favorite foods. As a result, God sent serpents to bite the people. Then God directed Moses to erect the bronze serpent, which would protect the people if they looked upon it (Num. 21:5–9).

- When the people of Israel began to commit adultery with the women of Moab and began to worship their gods, God again sent a plague that destroyed twenty-four thousand Israelites (Num. 25:1–9).

Eight times the Israelite people brought on the wrath of God because of their murmuring and complaining and disobedience. What a powerful illustration of the truth that the power of life and death is in the tongue (Prov. 18:21).

Remember that when the children of Israel began their journey to the Promised Land, the Lord said an angel would go before them. God warned the people not to offend this angel of the Lord because if they did, the angel would stop them from inheriting the land. (See Exodus 23:20–21 and Judges 2:1–4.) For a moment, think about how many people of God today fall into the trap of complaining about a ministry, a preacher, or other Christians, and as a result, the blessings of God are withheld in their lives or in their church.

Let me tell you of one example from my father's ministry. My father pastored a church in Bailey's Crossroads, Virginia, which he grew from ten members to more than one hundred twenty-five. In the early days of his ministry there, Dad had to work at another job part-time, and Mom had to work also because the church could not adequately support them. During that time, there was a man who served on the pastor's council.

The time came when the church was able to give Dad a salary. When that happened, this man on the council began to complain about the need to pay my dad a salary. One day while this man was at home, as he stood near an open window, all of a sudden two hands struck him between the shoulders and knocked him down. His head hit the radiator and knocked out his front teeth.

Because there was no one in the house but this man and his wife, at first he thought it must have been his wife! However, she was busy sewing in another room. He had to go to the hospital and get stitches. He was very frightened because he realized actual physical hands had struck him.

Let me help you understand what I believe happened to this man by giving an example from God's Word. In Luke 16:19–31 we have the story of the rich man in hell who pleaded with Abraham to allow Lazarus to "dip the tip of his finger in water and cool my tongue; for I am tormented in this flame" (v. 24, NKJV). I've always wanted to know why he would say his tongue was tormented. Well, if you will go to the story, you will see that before the rich man went to hell, a poor man was sitting at the foot of his table trying to catch the crumbs that fell while the rich man ate. The very thing that represented what he used to withhold help to this poor man—his mouth eating food—was the thing that God judged to burn throughout eternity. He could have used his mouth to help someone else, and he didn't. Perhaps if he had refused to give money to the poor man, the back of his hip would have burned because of his greed.

In another example from my dad's ministry, a woman in his church created contention during a business meeting. While my dad was speaking, this woman stood up and started shouting, "Come out of him, you devil!"

At first my dad thought it must be a CB radio system and turned around to see this woman standing up. He asked, "Who are you talking to, woman?"

She said, "I'm talking to you."

"Who are you calling a devil?" he asked.

She said, "I'm calling you a devil."

My dad's left hand began to shake under the power of God. He began to pray in tongues and rebuke the spirit of the enemy. As a result, this woman walked out of the church.

The next day that woman could not speak at all. She remained unable to speak for nearly a year. She went to the doctor, and the doctor said, "There is no explanation for this. We cannot find anything wrong with your vocal cords. You have simply gone totally dumb." He told her it would cost her thousands of dollars to travel to New Orleans to see a specialist and try to find out what happened to her voice. Her condition continued for several more months.

Then one day the Lord spoke to my dad and said, "Now, Fred, this woman is proud and is not going to repent for what she said to you. But her children need her. I will heal her if you are willing to stand in the gap and tell her that you release her and forgive her."

Shortly after this, while I was in revival there, the woman

attended the service. When my dad saw her, he asked her to come up to the front. He also called my mother to the front. Quietly, he told her that because she was proud and would not repent, she had not been healed yet. But God had told him that if he and my mother would forgive her and stand in the gap for her, God would heal her. My dad and mother assured her that they had forgiven her.

The next morning at six o'clock, the woman was totally healed. However, she never repented, if you can believe that. Her house burned down twice. She and her husband had marital problems. Recently my dad found out that she had been killed in a horrific car accident. I believe the woman would not have suffered the way she did if she had not offended the Holy Spirit by offending my father.

Because my dad forgave her and released her in the spirit realm, she was healed. He understands the spiritual realm and does not walk in bitterness and unforgiveness. However, she had also offended the Holy Spirit, and because you should not offend the Holy Spirit, God allowed a very swift judgment to come to her.

2. Unbelief will offend the angels.

Let me give you another example from God's Word of how the angel of the Lord can bring judgment upon you. In Luke 1:8–20, Zacharias the priest was about to administer prayers upon the golden altar. As he walked into the holy of holies before the altar, he saw an angel standing at the right side of the altar. (See Luke 1:5–23.) Tradition says that if the priest saw an angel of the Lord on the right side of the altar, it meant that God had come down. It was a very serious moment, and the priest could be struck dead by the presence of God. Zacharias was filled with fear. No one else was permitted to come in, so he knew it was not another priest.

The angel said to him, "You are going to have a son. He is going to be named John. He is going to go before the Lord and is going to come in the spirit of Elijah." (See Luke 1:13–17.)

Now, that is very detailed information. Zacharias should have praised God and said, "Thank You for coming. We have been praying for a family." But does he say that? No, he says, "How shall I know that? Give me a sign." (See verse 18.)

The angel of the Lord was offended, and he said, "You will be mute and not able to speak until the day these things take place, because you did not believe my words" (v. 20, NKJV). Unbelief can offend an angel of God.

How different is the story of Mary in Luke 1:26–38! An angel appeared to Mary and said, "And behold, you will conceive in your womb and bring forth a Son, and shall call His name JESUS. He will be great, and will be called the Son of the Highest" (vv. 31–32, NKJV). Once again, an angel appears to tell Mary she will have a boy named Jesus, and he tells her His destiny and purpose. Now, if anyone should have doubted, Mary should have doubted. She was just a young girl, possibly fourteen or fifteen, and not even married. She should be the one to say, "Look, maybe you have the wrong house. I'm not even married."

Instead, she said to the angel, "Let it be to me according to your word" (v. 38, NKJV). That is faith. She was honored as a woman of great faith because she believed what the angel told her.

It is clear that unbelief can offend the angel of God. That is the whole story of the children of Israel. If you will read Exodus and Numbers, you will see that the nation of Israel offended the angel of the Lord over and over again. Zacharias, a priest of God, should have believed the angel's words and not doubted, yet he doubted. Mary, a young virgin girl, heard a message that seemed impossible, but she believed.

God does not honor unbelief. For God to honor our unbelief would be totally contrary to the law of faith, for the Bible says, "Without faith it is impossible to please [God]" (Heb. 11:6, NKJV). The Bible says that it was the unbelief of the people of Nazareth that prevented Jesus from being able to do mighty works in that city—His hometown (Matt. 13:58). In Matthew 17:20, the disciples were unable to cast evil spirits out of a little boy, and Jesus gave only one reason—because of their unbelief. He said, "This kind does not go out except by prayer and fasting" (v. 21, NKJV). That could mean this kind of evil spirit or this kind of unbelief— the only way you could get rid of your unbelief was by prayer and fasting. God does not honor unbelief. Unbelief can literally stop the blessings of God.

Unbelief can offend the angel of God. Unbelief can hinder healing; unbelief can stop the blessings of God in general. We must be careful what we say and how we say it.

3. Sin will offend your angel.

In John 5:1–15 we find the story of the lame man who had been lying at the pool of Bethesda for thirty-eight years, waiting to be the first in the water when the angel came and stirred the waters. When Jesus saw him lying there, He immediately told him, "Rise, take up your bed and walk" (v. 8, nkjv). The man was immediately healed. Jesus then said to him, "See, you have been made well. Sin no more, lest a worse thing come upon you" (v. 14, nkjv). A person can be forgiven and set free of a sin, but if they go back into sin, it will open the door for that particular sin to come back upon them.

When we speak of sin, we think of adultery, fornication, lying, murder, stealing, and so forth. But remember that offending with your words—complaining, criticizing, and speaking negative things of the Spirit of God—is also a sin, and you will be judged accordingly.

At one time I was preaching a revival that continued for three weeks. One night a man came up to me whom I had seen in the services night after night. He always quoted a scripture to me when I spoke with him, and I thought this man must be a man of faith. He said to me, "Preacher, I want you to pray for me. I'm going deaf in both ears."

I asked, "Why are you going deaf? Can they tell you why you are going deaf?"

"Nope," he answered, "they can't tell me why I'm going deaf. But I want a miracle." He started quoting healing scriptures to me.

So I put my fingers in his ears and started to pray. As I began, the Holy Spirit said to me, "Get your fingers out of his ears. He has offended Me." I thought, "What in the world?" Why had the

Lord stopped me? I thought, "Let me try this again," and I tried the spirits to see what was going on.

The Lord spoke to me again in my spirit. "This man has complained about the music in this church and about the choruses they sing, and he has offended Me. Since he doesn't like the music, I'm going to let him go deaf so he won't hear it anymore and complain." I told the man what the Lord had told me.

He protested and tried to say, "I don't know anything about that."

I told him, "Don't you lie to the Holy Spirit. You've spoken evil about some of the music of this church." This made him mad, and he went back and sat down and folded his arms.

After the service, I told the pastor what had happened. He said, "You said what? You told the man that?"

"Yes, I did," I answered. "I told the man what the Spirit of God had said to me."

The pastor said, "But I hadn't told you anything about that man."

I said, "No, you didn't. But was I in order? If I wasn't in order, I'm going to apologize to the man."

Then the pastor told me, "When I brought my new music director in, that man would sit on the front row and put cotton in his ears. The cotton would hang down all the way to his neck. And he would stand up, face the church, and show them that he didn't like the music."

I said, "Let me tell you something, Pastor. The Lord spoke to me and told me he had offended the church and the pastor, and as a result, he wouldn't get healed."

Here is the good thing you can learn from this story. The Lord gives you an opportunity to repent and come clean with your sin. But that man never came back and apologized. He never owned up to his spiritual pride and would not believe that it was the Holy Spirit at work in his life.

One time when I was preaching a revival, my brother and his wife told me the story of a man in their church. I was teaching on worship. One of the verses in the Bible that I used speaks about dancing before the Lord. I explained what that meant. There was an old man in the church who loved the Lord but didn't believe in dancing before the Lord. Like many other people, he was a good man doing everything right in many areas but still missing the point in just one area—and it was costing him.

This old man said, "I don't believe all that. When people get up and jump up and down, that is all of the devil. God don't do things like that."

Immediately following that statement, he began experiencing pains in his feet and below his ankles. Eventually, he had to have his toes and part of his foot amputated. He got to the point that he couldn't walk, couldn't stand up and shout if he wanted to, because of the condition of his feet.

It's not that God is out there trying to judge everybody and inflict them with disease and judgment. We can go back to the children of Israel to understand this principle. When the Israelites offended the angel of God, God took down the hedge of protection from around them, and they began to be attacked by their enemies. When we offend the angel of the Lord, the same thing happens. When we offend the Holy Spirit or the angel of God, then He cannot defend us and bring us healing as in the story of the man at the pool of Bethesda. He cannot step in and intervene in our situation. We can bind the presence of God, bind the protection from the angel of God, by the very things that we say or do.

Sin will offend the angel of God.

4. Not giving God the glory can offend the angel of the Lord.

This story is told in Acts 12:1–2, 20–25, of King Herod, who killed James, a wonderful apostle of Christ. When he saw how pleased the Jews were by this act, he imprisoned Peter and planned to kill him also. However, due to the protection of his own angel, Peter escaped from prison.

Shortly after this, King Herod appeared before all the people dressed in regal garments and sitting upon a throne. Josephus describes Herod as dressed in a garment covered with silver from his neck down. When the sun hit the silver of his garment, it glowed, and the people began to shout, saying, "[It's] the voice of a god and not of a man!" (v. 22, NKJV). Herod did nothing to stop the shouts of the people, and the Bible says, "Then immediately an angel of the Lord struck him, because he did not give glory to God. And he was eaten by worms and died" (v. 23, NKJV).

Understand what this is saying: Herod wasn't killed because he killed James or because he arrested Peter. He was struck down by the Lord because "he did not give glory to God." In *Antiquities of the Jews*, book 19, chapter 8, section 2, Josephus expands on this story by giving more details about what happened to Herod, saying that he fell into the deepest of sorrows, a severe pain arose in his bowels, and he died after several days.

An angel of the Lord smote Herod. I believe the angel that released Peter from prison was likely the same angel that brought judgment to Herod.

Not giving God the glory can bring offense to the angel of God.

5. Disobedience to the Word can offend your angel.

In Numbers 22 we find the story of Balaam. He was a seer and a great prophet who had great power. He could prophesy things that were going to come to pass. In this chapter, messengers of Moab came to Balaam, and they said, "Look, we'll pay any amount of money you want to stand on the mountain and curse these people." Two times God admonished Balaam not to go with the men and do as they asked. The third time they asked, Balaam went with them. As he was riding on his donkey, an angel appeared in front of the donkey. The Lord opened the donkey's eyes to see the angel, and in fear the donkey stepped aside and, in doing so, crushed Balaam's foot against the wall. In anger, Balaam began beating the donkey.

The angel began to speak through the donkey's mouth to Balaam—almost like a ventriloquist would speak through his puppet. Now, if a donkey began talking to me and rebuking me, I'd jump off that donkey, go home, call Barnum and Bailey circus, and say, "Look I've got a talking donkey. I mean, the dude talks!"

Who is going to start fussing with a donkey? But Balaam got off the donkey and started arguing with the donkey.

Finally, the angel of the Lord heard and severely rebuked Balaam, saying, "Why have you struck your donkey these three times? Behold, I have come out to stand against you, because your way is perverse before Me. The donkey saw Me and turned aside from Me these three times. If she had not turned aside from Me, surely I would also have killed you by now, and let her live" (vv. 32–33, NKJV).

The angel of the Lord stood there in front of the donkey to resist the blessing of Balaam, to resist the prophecies of Balaam, because he had a very perverse way. There was something about him that just was not right.

ANYONE CAN OFFEND AN ANGEL

Let me make this point: good people who love the Lord can still offend their angels in some of the five ways I've listed.

Moses was the meekest man in all the earth. Moses is listed among the Jewish people as being one of the greatest men who ever lived, along with Elijah, yet Moses offended the angel of the Lord even after God told him not to.

In the story of Moses leading the people to the Promised Land, after they had been wandering in the wilderness for a very long time—thirty-eight years—the people were still complaining. They said to Moses, "Why have you brought up the assembly of the LORD into this wilderness, that we and our animals should die here?... It is not a place of grain or figs or vines or pomegranates; nor is there any water to drink" (Num. 20:4–5, NKJV). Moses and Aaron left the complaining people, went into the tabernacle, and fell on their faces before the Lord, asking His help once again. God responded to their prayer and told them, "Take the rod; you and your brother Aaron gather the congregation together. Speak to the rock before their eyes, and it will yield its water; thus you shall bring water for them out of the rock, and give drink to the congregation and their animals" (v. 8, NKJV).

I've heard many preachers say that the reason Moses was not allowed to go into the Promised Land was because he struck the rock two times instead of merely speaking to it as the Lord had instructed him. I believed that was true until I traveled to the country of Jordan and heard our Christian Arab tour guide give his explanation.

He took us to Numbers 20:10, where Moses and Aaron were aggravated with the people. They were always complaining, they were always negative, and now they wanted water from the rock. Moses said, "Hear now, you rebels! Must we bring water for you out of this rock?" (NKJV). After thirty-eight long years in the wilderness, Moses was growing pretty frustrated with the complaints of the people. In verse 11, Moses hits the rock two times instead of speaking to it.

Because of his disobedience, God tells Moses, "Because you did not believe Me, to hallow Me in the eyes of the children of Israel, therefore you shall not bring this assembly into the land which I have given them" (v. 12, NKJV). It is right after this incident that Aaron, the high priest, dies (vv. 24–26).

I now believe that the reason God told Moses, "You are going to die short of the Promised Land, and you are not going to be able to enter the Promised Land" was just as God states in verse 12: Moses did not "hallow Me in the eyes of the children of Israel." In other words, Moses did not tell the people it would be the Lord who brought water out of the rock. He did not give the glory to God, saying instead, "Must we bring water for you out of this rock?"

I believe that at times there are people who do not receive the things they need from the Lord because their motives for receiving these things are not right. Someone may say, "O God, I want You to bless me, and if You do, I will be a giver." But they aren't already givers and don't really intend to become a giver if God blesses them. Others may not receive from the Lord because He knows they do not intend to give Him the glory.

WHAT TO DO IF YOU HAVE OFFENDED THE ANGEL OF THE LORD

There are three things you should do if you feel that somehow you have really offended God:

- *Confess your sin.* Pray, "Lord, I have really done wrong." Don't wait for someone to come to you and ask you to forgive them. Confess your sin before God.

- *Repent.* Repent means more than merely confessing your sin. Repent means to turn. Tell the Lord that with His help you are not going to do the things that offended Him anymore. Turn from your sin, and commit to do your best to walk with Him daily.

- *Ask God to help you to forgive others who have wronged you, and find a way to restitution with that person.* In other words, write a letter to that person if you cannot physically see him or her. Tell him that although the situation may have happened years earlier, you have asked God to forgive you for your unforgiving spirit, and now you are asking that person to forgive you. This is an extremely important step to take, especially if you need healing.

I recently heard a young man in Cleveland, Tennessee, give a testimony. He had been in a wheelchair for many years. Many people had prayed for him, but he had not been healed. He said this: "I finally got into a meeting where the power of God was moving." He said that he simply humbled himself before God. He quit being bitter with God. He quit asking God why he wasn't healed. The power of God hit him, and he got out of that wheelchair and walked. The key was that he humbled himself before

God. You can never go wrong by humbling yourself before God and saying, "Lord, I need Your help." God will honor your faith; He will honor your integrity.

If we walk faithfully with God, all of God's presence, all of God's power, and all of the blessings of God will be ours.

A FINAL WORD

By James W. Goll

*G*ENESIS 28 RECORDS a time when heaven opened up and visitors came down for an earthly visit. They revealed God's intentions, and they made promises (and the promises came true). Who could have imagined?

The man who was privileged to receive the angelic visitors did not seem to deserve such a high honor. As a matter of fact, his character was seriously flawed. He had conspired with his mother, cheated his older brother, and even deceived his ailing father. The night the angels came down, he was running like a fugitive from his home, from his God, and from his own true calling, destiny, and identity. The night with the angels changed all that.

Jacob was destined to become the father of the twelve great tribes of Israel, but he was on the run from Beersheba to Haran, which was twelve miles north of Jerusalem. Night fell, so he found a rock for a pillow and, exhausted, sank into a deep sleep. He began to dream. Now, you might think that having gone off to sleep in such a disturbed condition, he might have had nightmares, full of tension and anxiety. God would have been justified in giving him dreams full of stern admonitions about honesty, truthfulness, and obedience, dreams that would have warned him about the certain penalty for his enormous sins.

Instead, a gracious God gave Jacob a glimpse of heaven coming down to earth. This man named Jacob, who was a deceiver and a supplanter, saw a sight that few others have seen. God's own illumination lit up the darkness, stretching from heaven to earth and back again. Jacob beheld the transcendent beauty of the Lord God.

Ministering angels—too many to count—moved down and up on a heavenly ladder or staircase.

Jacob was blown away. He had had an encounter with God Himself, who stood at the top of the heavenly ladder, directing everything so that the generational blessing and destiny He had promised to Jacob's grandfather would be fulfilled.

Jacob experienced an authentic heavenly encounter, and it changed him overnight. Now he was humbled by a holy awe; his stony sleeping place had become a tabernacle for the glory of God, his pillow an altar of remembrance.

Jacob's experience is unique in all of history. Yet *Jacob's ladder keeps coming down* from heaven. The true stories in this book are only a small sampling of the number of "ladders" that have come down from heaven into the lives of ordinary people like you and me.

We are not alone. We have a *lot* more angelic company than we realize most of the time. Unending worship proceeds from this angelic choir to the One who sits upon the throne. God's manifest presence, plans, and purposes keep on tumbling down into a time space world.

When we pray, "Thy kingdom come, Thy will be done on earth as it is in heaven," we are welcoming heaven's hosts to come and join us, aid us, and strengthen us. We can partner with heaven to bring about God's kingdom agenda on the earth. His angelic hosts are ready to come and release wisdom, revelation, comfort, and direction. We need only to align with God's Word, submit to His authority, and welcome His supernatural provision.

Let's pray:

> *Lord, we welcome Your angels, Your messengers. We welcome them however they may come, whether in fire or wind or without any sound at all. We say, as Your people have said through all the ages, "We need help from heaven." We need to be strengthened. We call forth once again for Jacob's ladder to come down into our earth realm. Lord, we long to see Your will done in the earth. Use us to fulfill Your plans. Impart to us the wisdom*

of heaven. It's all about You. It's not about us, and it's not even about Your angels. It's Your kingdom that's coming, Lord. Fulfill Your promises. Execute Your end-time plans! We stand before You, as ready as we can be. Prepare us; make us part of Your army; keep us alert and responsive to You. We love You! In Jesus's name, amen.

NOTES

INTRODUCTION

1. C. H. Spurgeon, "The First Christmas Carol," sermon, Music Hall, Royal Surrey Gardens, Kennington, London, December 20, 1857, http://www.spurgeon.org/sermons/0168.htm (accessed January 13, 2015).

CHAPTER 1 — WHAT ARE ANGELS?

1. C. Fred Dickason, *Angels: Elect and Evil* (Chicago: Moody Press, 1975), 58

2. Lehman Strauss, *Demons Yes—But Thank God For Good Angels* (Neptune, NJ: Loizeaux Brothers, 1976), 88.

3. Henry Clarence Thiessen, *Lectures in Systematic Theology* (Grand Rapids, MI: William B. Eerdmans Publishing Co., 1986), 134.

4. Robert Lightner, *Evangelical Theology* (Grand Rapids, MI: Baker Book House, 1986), 138, 135.

5. Scripture tells us that the sons of God saw that the daughters of men were beautiful, and the results of these unions were the Nephilim (Gen. 6:1–2, 4). It would seem that some fallen angels transgressed not only by taking on human bodies but by operating in all of the functions of those bodies, including sex. This transgression was so much worse than even rebellion against God that they were chained in darkness before the flood or at the time of the flood. Second Peter 2:4–5 indicates that these angels are "in the lowest part of Hades," apparently a sort of jail for holding prisoners awaiting judgment. The presence of the Nephilim does not change the fact that angels are not a race but a created order that were not designed to marry and have offspring.

6. Thiessen, *Lectures in Systematic Theology*, 134, 139.

7. John Ronner, *Do You Have a Guardian Angel?* (Murfreesboro, TN: Mamre Press, 1985), 153.

8. Charles Hunter and Francis Hunter, *Angels on Assignment* (New Kensington, PA: Whitaker House, 1979), 45.

9. Pascal Parente, *Beyond Space* (Rockford, IL: TAN Books and Publishers, 1973), 24.

10. Hope Price, *Angels* (London: Macmillian, 1993), 120.

11. Billy Graham, *Angels, God's Secret Agents* (Dallas: Word Publishing, 1986), 34–35.

12. Dickason, *Angels: Elect and Evil*, 43.

13. Sophy Burnham, *Angel Letters*, (New York: Ballantine Publishing Group, 1991), 123–127

14. Lewis Chafer, *Systematic Theology* (Grand Rapids, MI: Kregel Publications, 1993), 23.

CHAPTER 2 — THE NATURE OF ANGELS

1. Parente, *Beyond Space: A Book About Angels*, 18–19.

2. Martin Luther, *Table Talk*, trans. William Hazlitt (Gainesville, FL: Bridge-Logos, 2004), sec. 565.

3. John Calvin, *Institutes of the Christian Religion,* trans. Henry Beveridge (Grand Rapids, MI: Wm. B. Eerdmans Publishing Co., 1989), 1.14.5, 6, 9.

4. Margaret Barker, *An Extraordinary Gathering of Angels* (London: MQ Publications, 2004), 10.

5. Graham, *Angels: God's Secret Agents*, 30.

6. *Encyclopedia Mythica Online,* s.v. "angels" (by Rabbi Geoffrey W. Dennis), http://www.pantheon.org/articles/a/angels.html (accessed March 3, 2015).

7. Danny Steyne, "Angels in Bennington, Vermont," GreatestAwakening.com, http://www.greatestawakening.com/angelsinbennington .htm (accessed October 9, 2006). Used with permission.

8. Ibid.

9. Ibid.

CHAPTER 3 — THE CHARACTERISTICS OF ANGELS

1. *Catholic Encyclopedia Online,* s.v. "angels," http://www.new advent.org/cathen/01476d.htm (accessed January 14, 2015).

2. Ibid.; Thomas Aquinas, *Summa Theologica*, rev. ed., trans. Fathers of the English Dominican Province, 1.108, http://www .newadvent.org/summa/1108.htm (accessed March 3, 2015).

3. According to the *Catholic Encyclopedia Online,* "The only Scriptural names furnished of individual angels are Raphael, Michael, and Gabriel, names which signify their respective attributes. Apocryphal Jewish books, such as the Book of Enoch [and Esdras], supply those of Uriel and Jeremiel, while many are found in other apocryphal sources, like those Milton names in 'Paradise Lost.'"

4. Anna Rountree, *The Heavens Opened* (Lake Mary, FL: Charisma House, 1999).

5. You can read the Book of Enoch online by going to http://www .heavennet.net/writings/the-book-of-enoch/ (accessed January 14, 2015).

6. Coptic Orthodox Church Network, "The Coptic Church and Dogmas," 3.2, http://www.copticchurch.net/topics/thecopticchurch/ church3-2.html (accessed March 3, 2015).

CHAPTER 4 — ANGELS IN THE LIVES OF GOD'S PEOPLE

1. Norvel Hayes, *Putting Your Angels to Work* (Tulsa, OK: Harrison House, 1989), 8, 23.

2. Fred H. Wight, *Manners and Customs of Bible Lands* (Chicago: Moody Press, 1953), 112–113.

3. Marilyn Hickey, *Angels All Around* (Denver, CO: Marilyn Hickey Ministries, 1991), 131–132.

CHAPTER 5 — ANGELS IN THE LIFE OF JESUS

1. Hal Lindsey, *Satan Is Alive and Well on Planet Earth* (Grand Rapids, MI: Zondervan, 1972), 55.

2. John MacArthur Jr., *God, Satan, and Angels* (Panorama City, CA: Word of Grace Publications, 1983), 123; A. C. Gaebelein, *What the Bible Says About Angels* (Grand Rapids, MI: Baker Book House, 1993), 9–10.

3. Graham, *Angels, God's Secret Agents*, 121.

4. Lindsey, *Satan Is Alive and Well*, 54.

5. Hickey, *Angels All Around*, 17.

6. James Strong, *Strong's Exhaustive Concordance of the Bible* (Nashville, TN: Thomas Nelson, 1990), Greek dictionary, #1247.

7. Guy Duffield and Nathaniel Van Cleave, *The Foundations of Pentecostal Theology* (Los Angeles: L.I.F.E. Bible College, 1983), 485–486.

8. There are some discrepancies between the four Gospels about how many angels were at Jesus's tomb and exactly where they were. The answer may be that all of the accounts are accurate, just reported from the perspective of different people.

9. As quoted in Roy H. Hicks, *Guardian Angels* (Tulsa, OK: Harrison House, 1991), 5.

CHAPTER 6 — ANGELS AND THE NATION OF ISRAEL

1. The twenty-four books of the Hebrew Bible (Tanakh) that became the Old Testament of our Christian Bible include the five Books of Moses (the Pentateuch, or Torah)—Genesis, Exodus, Leviticus, Numbers, and Deuteronomy; eight Books of the Prophets— Joshua, Judges, Samuel (1 and 2 Samuel), Kings (1 and 2 Kings),

Isaiah, Jeremiah, Ezekiel, and The Twelve (Trei-Assar) or the minor prophets; and eleven Books of the Writings—Psalms, Proverbs, Job, Song of Songs, Ruth, Lamentations, Ecclesiastes, Esther, Daniel, Ezra, Nehemiah, and Chronicles (1 and 2 Chronicles). The twelve books of the minor prophets include Hosea, Joel, Amos, Obadiah, Jonah, Micah, Nahum, Habakkuk, Zephaniah, Haggai, Zechariah, and Malachi. The Hebrew Books of Samuel, Kings, Ezra/Nehemiah, and Chronicles are each divided into two books in the Christian Bible.

2. This information comes from Appendix 2 of Gary Kinnaman, *Angels Dark and Light* (Ann Arbor, MI: Servant/Vine, 1994), 221.

3. Lance Lambert, *Battle for Israel* (Eastbourne, East Sussex, England: Kingsway Publications, 1975), 9, 13–14.

4. Ibid., 111.

5. Bill Yount, "The 'Esthers' Are Now Being Summoned to Come to Jerusalem to Stand Before the King…for Such a Time as This," on The Elijah List, August 18, 2006, http://www.elijahlist.com/words/display_word/4395 (accessed January 15, 2015).

CHAPTER 7 — ANGELS WORSHIP GOD

1. John Paul Jackson, *7 Days Behind the Veil* (North Sutton, NH: Streams Publishing House, 2006), 28–29.

CHAPTER 8 — ANGELS PROTECT US

1. Bill Bright, "Guardian Angels Watching Over Us," Angel Stories and Miracles, http://www.thoughts-about-god.com/angels/bb_guardian.htm (accessed January 16, 2015).

2. FOXNews.com, "Caught on Camera," *FOX and Friends*, December 25, 2008, http://www.foxnews.com/video-search/m/21712317/caught_on_camera.htm (accessed January 16, 2015).

CHAPTER 10 — ANGELS STRENGTHEN US

1. "Angel Comes to Encourage," Angel Stories and Miracles, http://www.thoughts-about-god.com/angels/surgery.htm (accessed January 16, 2015).

CHAPTER 11 — ANGELS FIGHT FOR US

1. Kenneth E. Hagin, *The Triumphant Church* (Tulsa, OK: Harrison House, 1994), 208–209.

2. Duffield and Van Cleave, *Foundations of Pentecostal Theology*, 508–509.

3. W. E. Vine, Merrill F. Unger, and William White Jr., *Vine's Expository Dictionary of the Old and New Testaments* (Nashville, TN: Thomas Nelson, 1985), s.v. "wrestle, wrestling."

4. Judson Cornwall and Michael Reid, *Whose War Is It Anyway?* (Essex, England: Sharon Publications, 1993), 14, 17.

5. Ibid., 16.

6. Hagin, *The Triumphant Church*, 244.

7. Neil Anderson, *Victory Over the Darkness* (Ventura, CA: Regal Books, 1990), 54.

8. Hagin, *The Triumphant Church*, 150.

9. Otis, "An Overview of Spiritual Mapping," in Breaking Strongholds, Wagner ed., 36–37.

CHAPTER 12 — ANGELS EXECUTE JUDGMENT

1. Jim Bramlett, "Angels Discovered Singing End-Time Song in Rural Chinese Worship Service in 1995!" http://www.virtualchurch .org/vchurch/angels.htm (accessed January 19, 2015).

CHAPTER 13 — THROUGH GOD'S COMMAND

1. Bart, "Switch Lanes Angel Story," Amazing Angel Stories, http:// www.angelrealm.com/switch_lanes_story/index.htm (accessed January 19, 2015).

CHAPTER 14 — THROUGH SCRIPTURE

1. Eugene Merrill, *New American Commentary: Deuteronomy* (Nashville, TN: B&H Publishing Group, 1994), 434–435.

CHAPTER 15 — THROUGH PRAYER

1. Adapted from "Prayed for God's Angels Story," Amazing Angel Stories, http://www.angelrealm.com/prayed_for_angels/index.htm (accessed March 3, 2015).

CHAPTER 16 — THROUGH KINGDOM MINISTRY

1. Terry Law, *The Truth About Angels* (Lake Mary, FL: Charisma House, 1994, 2006), 41–42.

2. Taken from the *Agape* Newsletter, Little Rock, AR, May/June, 1988, 3. This newsletter is published by Agape Church, pastored by Happy Caldwell, as related in Law, *The Truth About Angels*, 41.

3. Larry Libby, *Somewhere Angels* (Sisters, OR: Questar Publishers, 1994), 32, as related in Law, *The Truth About Angels*, 42.

4. Keyhole Ministries, "God's 26 Guards," http://keyholeministry.blogspot.com/2007/09/gods-26-guards.html (accessed January 20, 2015).

Chapter 17 — Five Biblical Principles That Release Angels

1. Neil Anderson, *The Bondage Breaker* (Eugene, OR: Harvest House Publishers, 1990), 61.

2. Buddy Harrison, *Understanding Authority for Effective Leadership* (Tulsa, OK: Harrison House, 1982), 21–46. Ralph Mahoney, "The Use and Abuse of Authority," *Acts* magazine, vol. 11, no. 4, 2–11.

3. Terry Law, *The Power of Praise and Worship* (Tulsa, OK: Victory House, 1981), 161–162.

4. Chafer, *Systematic Theology*, 73.

5. Ibid.

6. Cornwall and Reid, *Whose War Is It Anyway?*, 29.

A Final Word

1. Matthew Henry, *Matthew Henry's Commentary on the Whole Bible: New Modern Edition*, Electronic Database (Peabody, MA: Hendrickson Publishers, Inc., 1991), excerpted from commentary on Genesis 28.

EMPOWERED
TO RADICALLY CHANGE
YOUR WORLD

Charisma House brings you books, e-books, and other media from dynamic Spirit-filled Christians who are passionate about God.

Check out all of our releases from best-selling authors like **Jentezen Franklin**, **Perry Stone**, and **Kimberly Daniels** and experience God's supernatural power at work.

**CHARISMA
HOUSE**

www.charismahouse.com
twitter.com/charismahouse • facebook.com/charismahouse